Sweets and Puddings

Marshall Cavendish

Edited by Isabel Moore

Published by Marshall Cavendish Books Limited
58, Old Compton Street
London W1V 5PA

©Marshall Cavendish Limited, 1973, 1974, 1975,
1976, 1981

This material was first published by
Marshall Cavendish Limited
in the partwork *Supercook*

First printing 1976
Second printing 1981

Printed in Hong Kong

ISBN 0 85685 166 3

Contents

Key to symbols

☆ This is a guide to each recipe's preparation and cooking

    ☆ **Easy**

    ☆ ☆ **Requires special care**

☆ ☆ ☆ **Complicated**

① This is a guide to the cost of each dish and will, of course, vary according to region and season.

    ① **Inexpensive**

    ① ① **Reasonable**

① ① ① **Expensive**

⧖ This is a guide to the preparation and cooking time required for each dish and will vary according to the skill of the individual cook.

    ⧖ **Less than 1 hour**

    ⧖ ⧖ **1 hour to $2\frac{1}{2}$ hours**

⧖ ⧖ ⧖ **Over $2\frac{1}{2}$ hours**

Basic metric conversions

Solid measures

15 grams	=	$\frac{1}{2}$ ounce
25 grams	=	1 ounce
50 grams	=	2 ounces
125 grams	=	4 ounces
225 grams	=	8 ounces
450 grams	=	1 pound
1 kilogram	=	2 pounds 2 ounces

Liquid measures

25 millilitres	=	1 fluid ounce
50 millilitres	=	2 fluid ounces
125 millilitres	=	4 fluid ounces
150 millilitres	=	5 fluid ounces
300 millilitres	=	10 fluid ounces
600 millilitres	=	1 pint
1 litre	=	$1\frac{3}{4}$ pints

Linear measures

0·6 centimetre	=	$\frac{1}{4}$ inch
1·3 centimetres	=	$\frac{1}{2}$ inch
2·5 centimetres	=	1 inch
10 centimetres	=	4 inches
15 centimetres	=	6 inches
23 centimetres	=	9 inches
30 centimetres	=	1 foot
1 metre	=	40 inches

American equivalents of food and measurements are shown in brackets.

Sweets and puddings for the family

Desserts are the gilt on the gingerbread — not essential, exactly, but often the thing that makes cooking meals worthwhile. And when you've a young family to cater for, they are often the only food (with the possible exception of baked beans and fish fingers) for which enthusiasm is shown!

Desserts cover a whole range of eating experience, and this has been our prime consideration in selecting recipes for this book. So you will find filling, familiar dishes such as Apple Pie (page 322), lighter traditional dishes such as Fruit Fool (page 332), as well as elegant ones such as Chestnut Pudding (pictured below, recipe page 348). All are guaranteed to satisfy your most demanding family gourmet AND not to shatter your budget!

But of course there are times (birthdays, anniversaries and so on) when economy is not the order of the day and when you're quite prepared to stay in the kitchen for longer than usual. For times like these, something extra-special is called for, and these recipes are included in **For Special Occasions.** They MAY cost a bit more, they may take a bit more time to prepare, but they **will** make the most glorious finale to that special meal.

If it is the little luxuries that make life really worth living, you can't afford to ignore desserts.

Apple Fritters

This inexpensive and easy-to-make dessert is a favourite with children. Bananas, apricots and pineapple rings may also be used.

4 SERVINGS

4 oz. [1 cup] flour
⅛ teaspoon salt
2 egg yolks, plus 1 egg white
1 tablespoon cooking oil
5 fl. oz. [⅝ cup] milk
1 lb. cooking apples
   juice of 1 lemon
   castor sugar
4 oz. [½ cup] butter

Sift the flour and salt into a medium-sized mixing bowl. Make a well in the centre of the flour and put in the egg yolks, white and oil. With a wooden spoon, mix them, slowly incorporating the flour and gradually adding the milk. Mix to a smooth batter, then beat well. Cover and keep in a cool place for 30 minutes.

Peel and core the apples and slice into rings ¼-inch thick. Lay the rings on a plate and sprinkle with lemon juice and sugar.

In a large frying-pan, melt the butter over high heat. Using a skewer, dip the apple rings into the batter and drop them one by one into the hot butter. Cook the rings on both sides until they are golden brown. Arrange on a plate and dredge with castor sugar. Serve at once.

Apple Pie

Traditional Apple Pie differs from other pies in several ways. First, the pastry is made with a greater proportion of fat to flour than are other pie crusts. In the filling, the apples are cut in rather thick slices. The filling is spiced with cinnamon, allspice and nutmeg and thickened with cornflour [cornstarch]. In the United States, Apple Pie is frequently served warm with vanilla ice cream.

6 SERVINGS

PASTRY
10 oz. [2½ cups] flour
¼ teaspoon salt
4 oz. [½ cup] vegetable shortening
   or lard
2 oz. [¼ cup] butter
6 tablespoons iced water
1 tablespoon single [light] cream
FILLING
6 oz. [¾ cup] sugar
1 teaspoon ground cinnamon
¼ teaspoon ground allspice
¼ teaspoon grated nutmeg
1 tablespoon cornflour [cornstarch]

2 lb. cooking apples, peeled, cored
   and quartered and each quarter
   cut into 3 slices
1 tablespoon lemon juice
1 oz. [2 tablespoons] butter, cut into
   small pieces

Sift the flour and salt into a large mixing bowl. Add the vegetable shortening or lard and the butter. With your fingertips, rub the fats into the flour until the mixture resembles fine breadcrumbs. Add the water a little at a time, and stir the dough, using a knife, until it is firm and not sticky. Knead the dough gently until it is smooth. Wrap the dough in aluminium foil and place it in the refrigerator for 30 minutes, or until it is well chilled.

Grease the bottom and sides of a 9-inch deep pie dish with a little butter.

Divide the dough in half. On a floured board, roll out one half in a circle large enough to line the pie dish. Lift the dough on to the rolling pin and unroll it over the pie dish. With your fingers gently ease the dough into the dish without pulling or stretching the dough. Using a sharp knife trim the dough so that it is even with the outer rim of the pie dish.

Preheat the oven to fairly hot 375°F (Gas Mark 5, 190°C).

For the filling, blend the sugar, cinnamon, allspice, nutmeg and cornflour [cornstarch] in a large mixing bowl. Add the sliced apples and lemon juice and toss together thoroughly.

Fill the pie shell with the apple mixture, piling it higher in the centre. Although the filling may seem to be quite high it will shrink when it bakes. Dot the top of the filling with the remaining butter.

For the top crust, roll out the remaining half of the dough into a circle which is about ⅛-inch thick and about 12-inches in diameter.

Lift it up on the rolling pin and over the filling. With scissors, trim the top crust to within ¼-inch of the dish. Tuck the overhanging dough under the edge of the bottom crust all around the rim and then press down with your fingers to seal the two crusts and make a design.

Brush the dough with the cream. With the scissors, cut two small gashes in the centre of the top.

Bake the pie in the middle of the oven for 40 minutes or until the crust is golden brown. Serve at once.

Serve this traditional Apple Pie the way the Americans do—with dollops of delicious vanilla ice-cream for lunch or dinner.

Porridge Apples

This warming Scottish dessert is easy to make and very economical. Serve it with plenty of whipped cream or thick, hot custard.

6 SERVINGS

8 oz. [1 cup] plus 1 teaspoon butter, melted
8 oz. [2 cups] rolled oats
6 oz. [1 cup] soft brown sugar
¼ teaspoon salt
8 medium-sized cooking apples, peeled, cored and thinly sliced
5 fl. oz. [⅝ cup] water
1 large cooking apple, cored and thinly sliced
2 tablespoons strained apricot jam, warmed

Preheat the oven to moderate 350°F (Gas Mark 4, 180°C).

Using the teaspoon of butter, grease a large baking dish and set aside.

In a medium-sized mixing bowl, combine the oats, sugar, salt and the remaining butter, stirring well with a wooden spoon to blend.

Layer the oat mixture and apple slices in the prepared baking dish, beginning and ending with a layer of oat mixture. Carefully pour the water over the mixture.

Porridge Apples makes a nutritious and filling dessert.

Place the unpeeled apple slices decoratively over the top of the pudding and, using a pastry brush, brush them with the apricot jam.

Place the dish in the centre of the oven and bake for 40 to 50 minutes or until the top of the pudding is deep golden brown.

Remove the dish from the oven and serve immediately.

Apple Charlotte

This delicious hot pudding is perfect for family lunches or dinners.

4-6 SERVINGS

FILLING
2 oz. [¼ cup] plus 1 teaspoon butter
2 lb. cooking apples, peeled, cored and cut into quarters
2 oz. [¼ cup] sugar
the rind of 1 lemon
1 small loaf of bread, a day or two old, crusts removed and cut into as many thin slices as required
4 oz. [½ cup] butter, melted
castor sugar

SAUCE
5 tablespoons apricot jam

3 tablespoons water
2 tablespoons medium sherry

Preheat the oven to moderate 350°F (Gas Mark 4, 180°C). Lightly grease a charlotte mould or ovenproof dish with the teaspoon of butter.

Put the apples, sugar, lemon rind and remaining butter in a medium-sized saucepan and, stirring occasionally with a wooden spoon, simmer over low heat for 10 minutes or until the apples are very soft. (They should neither be completely whole nor completely mashed.) Discard the lemon rind.

Cut the bread slices in halves. Dip the halved slices in the melted butter and line the bottom and sides of the mould or dish, overlapping the slices slightly. Fill with the apple mixture and cover with a layer of bread slices dipped in melted butter. Sprinkle the pudding with castor sugar and bake in the oven for 40 minutes, or until the top is golden brown.

While the charlotte is baking, put the jam and water in a small saucepan. Stir and bring to the boil. Reduce the heat to low and simmer for 3 minutes. Remove from the heat and stir in the sherry.

After taking the apple charlotte from the oven, let it stand for a minute or two before turning it out on to a warmed serving dish. Pour the warm, but not hot, jam sauce over it and serve immediately.

Apricot Bourdaloue Tart

The sharp taste of the apricots in this dessert tart contrasts pleasantly with the sweet cream.

4-6 SERVINGS

PASTRY
4 oz. [1 cup] flour
⅛ teaspoon salt
2 teaspoons castor sugar
1 oz. [2 tablespoons] butter
2 tablespoons vegetable fat
1 egg yolk
½ to 1 tablespoon iced water

FILLING
2 egg yolks
2 oz. [¼ cup] castor sugar
   grated rind of 1 orange
1½ tablespoons each cornflour [cornstarch] and flour mixed
10 fl. oz. [1¼ cups] milk
1 egg white
14 oz. canned halved apricots
   or 1 lb. fresh apricots, halved, stoned and poached in syrup
1 oz. [¼ cup] roasted almonds, flaked

Preheat the oven to moderate 350°F (Gas Mark 4, 180°C).

Sift the flour and salt into a medium-sized mixing bowl. Add the sugar and mix. Using a table knife, cut the butter and vegetable fat into the flour. Using your fingertips, rub the fat into the flour until the mixture resembles fine breadcrumbs. Make a well in the centre of the mixture and add the egg yolk mixed with ½ tablespoon of iced water. To begin with, use the knife to mix the flour mixture with the egg yolk, then use your hands to knead the dough until it is smooth. Add more iced water if the dough is too dry. Pat the dough into a ball, cover and refrigerate for 15 minutes.

Roll out the dough to line a 7½-inch flan tin. Refrigerate for 10 minutes. Bake blind, covering the bottom with foil weighed down with dried beans, for 30 minutes.

To make the crème bourdaloue, in a medium-sized mixing bowl beat the egg yolks with half the sugar. Add the grated orange rind and the cornflour [cornstarch] and flour mixture and beat until smooth. Put the milk in a pan on moderate heat and bring to the boil. Just as it comes to the boil, pour it slowly, stirring all the time, over the egg mixture. Stir until smooth. Return the mixture to the pan and, stirring constantly, bring to the boil. Remove from the heat and cool.

In a small mixing bowl, beat the egg white with the remaining sugar until stiff. Fold it into the cooked mixture.

Drain the apricot halves. Put the syrup into a small pan and boil rapidly until it thickens. Cool and set aside.

Remove the pastry shell from the tin and place it on a serving dish. Put the crème bourdaloue into the middle of the pastry shell and smooth with a knife. Cover completely with the apricots, sprinkle with the almonds and brush with the reduced syrup. Serve.

Apricot Pudding

Apricot Pudding is a delightful blend of apricots and cream.

6 SERVINGS

1½ lb. apricots, halved and stoned
4 fl. oz. [½ cup] water
5 tablespoons sugar
¾ oz. gelatine
1 x 7-inch sponge cake
4 tablespoons apricot jam
4 tablespoons medium sherry
1 teaspoon vegetable oil
3 oz. [½ cup] pistachios, chopped
15 fl. oz. double cream [1⅞ cups heavy cream]
6 fl. oz. [¾ cup] milk

Preheat the oven to warm 325°F (Gas Mark 3, 170°C).

Place the apricots in an ovenproof dish and pour over the water. Sprinkle 4 tablespoons of the sugar over the apricots and place the dish in the oven. Cook the apricots for 40 minutes or until they are tender. Remove the dish from the oven. Transfer the apricots to a plate.

Pour the apricot cooking juices into a small saucepan and add the gelatine. Place the pan over low heat and cook, stirring constantly, for 2 to 3 minutes or until the gelatine has dissolved. Do not allow the liquid to boil. Remove the pan from the heat. Add the remaining sugar to the pan and stir until the sugar has dissolved. Set aside to cool.

Slice the sponge cake in half, horizontally, and spread the jam over the bottom half. Sandwich together again. Cut into 1-inch squares and place the squares in a mixing bowl. Pour over the sherry and set aside for 5 minutes.

With the oil, grease a 3-pint [2-quart] mould. Arrange the apricot halves and pistachios in the mould.

In a medium-sized mixing bowl, beat the cream with a wire whisk or rotary beater until it is thick but not stiff. Carefully fold in the milk and the apricot jelly [gelatin] mixture.

Pour half the cream mixture into the mould and chill in the refrigerator for 30 minutes or until it is set.

Remove the mould from the refrigerator. Place the sponge in the centre of the mould and pour the remaining cream mixture on top. Chill the mould in the refrigerator for 2 hours or until it has set completely.

Remove the mould from the refrigerator. Dip the mould quickly in hot water. Invert a serving dish over the mould and, grasping the two firmly together, reverse them. The mould should slide out easily. Serve immediately.

Super Apricot Bourdaloue Tart.

Black Bottom Parfait

These two-tiered chocolate and vanilla parfaits make a mouth-watering dessert for lunch or dinner. They are easy to make and most attractive.

6 SERVINGS

2 teaspoons cornflour [cornstarch]
16 fl. oz. [2 cups] milk
4 egg yolks
4 oz. [½ cup] plus 1 tablespoon castor sugar
8 oz. dark [semi-sweet] chocolate, melted in 3 tablespoons dark rum or coffee

1 teaspoon vanilla essence
½ oz. gelatine
2 fl. oz. [¼ cup] boiling water
5 fl. oz. double cream [⅝ cup heavy cream], chilled
2 egg whites
¼ teaspoon salt
¼ teaspoon cream of tartar
2 oz. plain dark chocolate caraque curls

In a heavy medium-sized saucepan, mix the cornflour [cornstarch] and the milk together and, stirring continuously, bring to the boil over moderate heat.

Reduce the heat to low and cook, stirring constantly, for 5 minutes. Remove from the heat and allow to cool.

In a small bowl, beat the egg yolks and 4 ounces [½ cup] of sugar with a whisk until the egg yolks have thickened and become pale yellow. When the milk mixture has cooled, gradually stir the beaten eggs into it. Replace the pan on low heat and cook, stirring continuously, for 5 minutes, or until the mixture is thick. Do not boil or it will curdle.

Pour about half this custard into a medium-sized bowl. Add the melted chocolate and ½ teaspoon of vanilla essence and stir until well blended. Taste the chocolate custard and, if it is not sweet enough, add a little more sugar. Spoon the chocolate custard into 4 parfait or sundae glasses. Put them in the refrigerator to chill.

Put the gelatine in a small saucepan. Add the boiling water and stir over low heat until the gelatine has completely dissolved. Add it, with the remaining vanilla, to the custard in the saucepan.

Pour the cream into a medium-sized bowl and beat it with a whisk or rotary beater until it thickens slightly. Fold this into the custard mixture.

Put the egg whites, salt and cream of tartar in a medium-sized bowl and, with a balloon whisk or rotary beater, beat the egg whites until they are foamy. Gradually add the tablespoon of castor sugar and continue beating until the egg whites are stiff.

With a metal spoon, fold the beaten egg whites into the custard mixture in the saucepan.

Pour this mixture on top of the chocolate custard in the parfait or sundae glasses. Put the glasses back in the refrigerator to chill for at least 4 hours.

When the parfaits are quite firm, decorate the tops with chocolate caraque and serve immediately.

Black Bottom Parfait—a rich dessert for any occasion.

Chocolate Mousse

A mouthwatering, rich dish, Chocolate Mousse makes a superb dinner dessert. You could use the egg whites to make chocolate meringues and serve them with the mousse.

4 SERVINGS

4 oz. dark [semi-sweet] cooking chocolate, broken into pieces
2 oz. [¼ cup] castor sugar
10 fl. oz. [1¼ cups] milk
4 egg yolks
3 tablespoons dark rum or brandy
10 fl. oz. double cream [1¼ cups heavy cream]

Place the chocolate, sugar and milk in a medium-sized heavy saucepan. Set the pan over moderately low heat and cook, stirring frequently, for 3 to 5 minutes, or until the chocolate has melted.

Remove the pan from the heat and set it aside. In a heatproof mixing bowl, beat the egg yolks together with a wire whisk or rotary beater. Gradually add the milk mixture, beating constantly.

Set the bowl in a pan half-filled with hot water. Set the pan over low heat and cook the mixture, stirring constantly with a wooden spoon, until it coats the back of the spoon.

Remove the pan from the heat. Lift the bowl out of the pan. Stir in the rum or brandy and set the custard aside to cool completely, stirring occasionally.

Pour the cream into a medium-sized mixing bowl. Using a wire whisk or rotary beater, beat the cream until it forms stiff peaks. Fold the cream into the cooled chocolate custard, blending it in thoroughly.

Pour the mixture into a chilled glass serving bowl or individual glasses and chill in the refrigerator for 4 hours before serving.

Chocolate and Rum Fondue

This is a very unusual dessert to serve for dinner. The fondue should be served with a selection of fruit such as pears and bananas or cake cut into small pieces. The fruit or cake is speared on dessert forks and dipped into the hot chocolate.

6-8 SERVINGS

8 oz. dark [semi-sweet] chocolate, broken into small pieces

This unusual Chocolate and Rum Fondue is guaranteed to make any meal extra-special!

6 tablespoons double [heavy] cream
2 tablespoons rum
2 oz. icing sugar [½ cup confectioners' sugar], sifted

In a small bowl set over a pan of hot water, melt the chocolate with the cream, stirring constantly with a wooden spoon. As soon as the chocolate has melted, remove the bowl from the heat. Stir in the rum and the sugar.

Pour the mixture into a fondue pot set over a small spirit lamp.

Ignite the spirit lamp and serve the fondue with the fruit or pieces of cake.

Easy to make, even easier to eat— that's creamy, mouth-watering Chocolate Mousse.

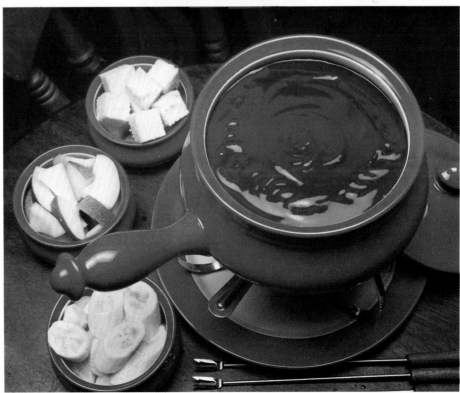

Clafoutis

FRENCH CHERRY PUDDING

This is the basic — and traditional — version of clafoutis. Clafoutis may be served on its own or with whipped cream or a light custard sauce.

6 SERVINGS

1 teaspoon margarine or butter
1¼ lb. fresh black cherries, washed and stoned or 1¼ lb. canned black cherries, stoned and drained
6 fl. oz. [¾ cup] milk
2 eggs
2 teaspoons vanilla essence
5 tablespoons icing [confectioners'] sugar
7 tablespoons flour
⅛ teaspoon salt

Preheat the oven to moderate 350°F (Gas Mark 4, 180°C). Grease a medium-sized baking dish with the teaspoon of margarine or butter.

Dry the black cherries thoroughly on kitchen paper towels and set aside.

In a large mixing bowl, blend the milk, eggs and vanilla essence, beating with a wire whisk until the liquid is smooth. Add 4 tablespoons of the sugar, 1 tablespoon at a time, whisking constantly, and make sure that each tablespoon has been

This traditional French Clafoutis is black cherries baked in batter. Serve with lots of custard or cream for a warming dessert.

absorbed before the next one is added. Add the flour, tablespoonful by tablespoonful in the same way, adding the salt with the final tablespoonful. When all the sugar and flour has been beaten in, the batter should be very smooth and of a very light pancake batter consistency.

Pour the batter into the greased baking dish and add the cherries, spreading them evenly throughout the batter. Bake in the centre of the oven for 50 minutes to 1 hour, or until a sharp knife inserted in the middle of the clafoutis comes out clean.

Remove the clafoutis from the oven, sprinkle the top of the pudding with the remaining icing [confectioners'] sugar and serve immediately.

Coriander Fruit Crumble

This unusual aromatic dessert is inexpensive, simple to make and has a very interesting flavour. Serve it for a family supper either hot or cold, with whipped cream or lots of custard.

4-6 SERVINGS

1 teaspoon butter
1½ lb. cooking apples, peeled, cored and thinly sliced
8 oz. fresh or frozen and thawed blackberries, washed
2 tablespoons soft brown sugar
1 teaspoon ground cinnamon
TOPPING
4 oz. [1 cup] flour
4 oz. [½ cup] sugar
4 oz. [½ cup] butter
2 teaspoons ground coriander

Preheat the oven to moderate 350°F (Gas Mark 4, 180°C). Lightly grease a 3-pint [2-quart] baking dish with the teaspoon of butter.

Put the apples and blackberries in the baking dish and sprinkle with the brown sugar and cinnamon.

To make the crumble topping, put the flour and sugar in a medium-sized mixing bowl. Add the butter and cut it into the flour with a table knife. Then using your fingertips, rub the butter into the flour and sugar until the mixture resembles coarse breadcrumbs. Mix in the ground coriander.

Sprinkle the crumble on top of the fruit and bake in the centre of the oven for 45 minutes.

Remove the baking dish from the oven and serve the crumble at once, if you are eating it hot.

Crème Caramel
BAKED CARAMEL CUSTARD

Crème Caramel is an exquisitely light dessert and, as it may be made in advance and chilled in the refrigerator, it is ideal to serve for a family dinner.

6 SERVINGS

CARAMEL
4 oz. [½ cup] sugar
2½ fl. oz. [¼ cup plus 1 tablespoon] water

CREME
1 pint [2½ cups] milk
3½ oz. [⅜ cup plus 1 tablespoon] sugar
½ vanilla pod or 1 teaspoon vanilla essence
2 eggs
2 egg yolks

To make the caramel, in a heavy, medium-sized saucepan, heat the sugar and water over low heat, stirring until the sugar dissolves completely. Increase the heat to moderately high and allow the syrup to come to the boil. Cook for 3 to 4 minutes, or until it turns a light golden brown in colour.

Be careful not to overcook the syrup or it will darken too much and become bitter. Immediately the caramel has reached the right colour, remove the pan from the heat and pour it into six individual ramekins or one heatproof dish. Do not allow the caramel to cool before pouring it into the ramekins or dish.

In a heavy, medium-sized saucepan bring the milk and sugar to the boil over moderate heat, stirring occasionally to dissolve the sugar. When the sugar has dissolved, add the vanilla pod to the milk. Cover the pan, remove from the heat and leave the vanilla to infuse with the milk for 20 minutes.

In a medium-sized mixing bowl, beat the eggs and the egg yolks with a wire whisk until they thicken and become pale yellow.

Beating continuously, gradually add the milk to the beaten eggs, pouring it in through a strainer. Discard the vanilla pod. If you have not used the vanilla pod, stir in the vanilla essence at this point. Stir well and pour the mixture into a large jug.

Preheat the oven to warm 325°F (Gas Mark 3, 170°C).

Pour the milk mixture through a silk

tammy or a very fine strainer into the six ramekins or the dish. Spoon off any froth which appears on the surface.

Place the dishes in a deep baking tin or bain marie and add enough boiling water to reach about half way up the sides of the dishes.

Place the baking tin or bain marie in the lower part of the oven and bake for 40 minutes, or until the centre of the crème is firm when pressed with your finger. Do not allow the water to simmer during the baking because if it does the custard will have a grainy texture. (If the water does begin to simmer, lower the oven heat immediately).

Remove the dish from the water and allow to cool thoroughly. Chill in the refrigerator for 1 hour. Then run a knife around the edge of the ramekins or dish and place a serving plate on top. Reverse the crème caramel on to it and serve immediately.

Cream Cheese Cake

A delicious cheesecake with an excitingly different spice flavour, Cream Cheese Cake is very easy to make and will be a great favourite with all the family! Serve as a special dessert for lunch and dinner or as a rich after-school or tea-time snack for the children.

ONE 9-INCH CAKE

2 oz. [¼ cup] plus 1 teaspoon butter, melted
6 oz. crushed digestive biscuits [1½ cups crushed graham crackers]
12 oz. cream cheese
6 oz. [¾ cup] sugar
1 egg, well beaten
1½ teaspoons ground ginger
12 fl. oz. [1½ cups] sour cream
4 tablespoons canned pineapple, drained and crushed

Preheat the oven to moderate 350°F (Gas Mark 4, 180°C). Lightly grease a 9-inch cake tin with the teaspoon of butter and set aside.

In a medium-sized mixing bowl, combine the digestive biscuits [graham crackers] and the remaining melted butter, beating until they are well blended. Spoon the mixture into the prepared cake tin and, using your fingers or a metal spoon, line the tin evenly with the mixture. Set aside.

In a medium-sized mixing bowl, combine the cream cheese, half of the sugar and the egg, beating with a fork until the mixture is smooth. Stir in 1 teaspoon of the ginger and mix well. Pour the mixture into the lined cake tin and place it in the centre of the oven. Bake for 25 to 30 minutes, or until the filling is set and firm to touch.

Meanwhile, in a large mixing bowl, combine the sour cream, the remaining sugar and the remaining ginger, beating briskly until the sugar has dissolved. Set aside.

Remove the cake from the oven and turn off the heat.

Spread the sour cream mixture evenly over the top of the cake and arrange the crushed pineapple on top. Return the tin to the oven and leave it there, with the door closed, for 5 minutes.

Remove the tin from the oven and place it in the refrigerator to chill for at least 1 hour.

Remove the tin from the refrigerator and serve cold, in small wedges.

Exquisite Creme Caramel is one of the shining glories of French cuisine —and its delicate taste is absolutely guaranteed to delight the entire family.

Flemish Strawberry and Almond Cake

A lovely dessert for a summer lunch or dinner, Flemish Strawberry and Almond Cake is surprisingly easy and economical to prepare.

6-8 SERVINGS

CAKE

3 oz. [¾ cup] plus 1 teaspoon butter, softened

2 oz. [½ cup] plus 2 teaspoons self-raising flour

3 oz. [⅜ cup] castor sugar

3 eggs

3 oz. [½ cup] ground almonds

FILLING

12 oz. strawberries, washed, hulled and puréed

2½ oz. icing sugar [½ cup plus 2 tablespoons confectioners' sugar]

5 fl. oz. double cream [⅝ cup heavy cream], whipped until stiff

¼ oz. gelatine dissolved in 1 tablespoon hot water

4 oz. strawberries, washed, hulled and halved

Preheat the oven to fairly hot 375°F (Gas

Scrumptious Flemish Strawberry and Almond Cake.

Mark 5, 190°C).

Lightly grease a round 7-inch cake tin with the teaspoon of butter. Sprinkle in the 2 teaspoons flour and tip and rotate the tin to distribute the flour evenly. Knock out any excess flour and set the tin aside.

In a medium-sized mixing bowl, cream the remaining butter and the sugar together with a wooden spoon until the mixture is fluffy. Beat in the eggs.

10

With a metal spoon, fold in the remaining flour and the ground almonds.

Turn the mixture into the prepared cake tin and place it in the centre of the oven.

Bake for 30 to 40 minutes, or until a skewer inserted into the centre of the cake comes out clean.

Remove the cake from the oven. Run a knife round the edge of the cake and reverse it onto a wire rack. Leave to cool.

Wash and thoroughly rinse out the cake tin.

To make the filling, in a medium-sized mixing bowl, combine the strawberry purée and 2 ounces [½ cup] of the sugar. Fold in the cream and then the dissolved gelatine. Turn the mixture into the dampened cake tin and place it in the refrigerator. Chill for 1 to 1½ hours or until the filling is set.

With a long sharp knife, slice the cake into two layers. Place one layer on a serving platter and turn out the strawberry filling on to it. Place the other cake layer on top.

Sift the remaining icing [confectioners'] sugar over the top of the cake and decorate with the strawberry halves.

Flummery

A traditional English sweet dish, Flummery makes a delicious family lunch or dinner dessert. Serve with lots of stiffly whipped cream or a mixed fresh fruit compôte.

4 SERVINGS

4 oz. [⅔ cup] round-grain rice, washed, soaked in cold water for 30 minutes and drained
10 fl. oz. [1¼ cups] milk
10 fl. oz. double cream [1¼ cups heavy cream]
2 oz. [¼ cup] sugar
1 tablespoon finely grated lemon rind
1 teaspoon ground cinnamon

Combine all the ingredients in the top part of a double saucepan. Half fill the bottom part with boiling water and place the double saucepan over moderately low heat. Cover the saucepan and cook the mixture, stirring occasionally, for 50 minutes to 1 hour, or until the rice is soft and tender and has absorbed most of the liquid.

Remove the pan from the heat and pour the mixture into a 1-pint [1½-pint] soufflé or other decorative serving dish. Allow the mixture to cool to room temperature, then place the dish in the refrigerator to chill for 3 hours, or until the flummery is set and firm.

Serve cold.

Ginger Pear Sauce

This is a sweet fruit sauce to serve with ice-cream or hot gingerbread for a super luncheon treat.

12 FLUID OUNCES [1½ CUPS]

14 oz. canned pear halves, drained, chopped and the syrup reserved
4 tablespoons evaporated milk
2 tablespoons finely chopped preserved ginger
1 tablespoon rum (optional)

Measure 8 fluid ounces [1 cup] of the pear syrup and pour it into a small saucepan. Add the evaporated milk and stir well. Place the pan over moderate heat and bring the liquid to the boil. Boil the syrup for 10 minutes or until it has reduced by one-third the original quantity.

Remove the pan from the heat and stir in the chopped pears, ginger and the rum if you are using it.

Serve the sauce immediately.

Traditional English Flummery has been a favourite all over Britain for centuries.

Fruit Fool

A fruit fool is one of the simplest and most delicious of all summer desserts. The two ingredients are simply fruit and cream. Custard may be substituted for the cream but the result is not nearly so good. Strawberries, gooseberries, raspberries, blackcurrants and apricots make the best fools — and of these, gooseberries, blackcurrants and apricots should be poached in a little water first until they are tender. The fruit should then be drained since the purée should be thick. Fruit fools may be served with sponge finger biscuits [cookies] or digestive biscuits [graham crackers].

4 SERVINGS

2 lb. fresh fruit, washed and hulled if necessary

10 fl. oz. double cream [1¼ cups heavy cream], lightly whipped

If necessary, poach the fruit first, then drain it. With a wooden spoon, mash the fruit through a strainer or purée it through a food mill into a large mixing bowl. Set the bowl aside and allow the purée to cool.

Lightly fold the whipped cream into the purée. Place the bowl in the refrigerator and chill for at least 2 hours.

Pour the fool into a serving dish and serve cold.

Hasty Pudding

Hasty Pudding, made from milk, flour, butter and spices, is an old English dessert, so named because it could be quickly prepared from the staple contents of the larder. Serve it with strawberry jam or golden [light corn] syrup for a family lunch or supper.

2-3 SERVINGS

2 oz. [¼ cup] plus 1 teaspoon butter
2 tablespoons flour
16 fl. oz. [2 cups] milk
½ teaspoon finely grated nutmeg
4 tablespoons soft brown sugar
½ teaspoon ground cinnamon

Preheat the grill [broiler] to high.

Lightly grease a medium-sized flame-proof baking dish with the teaspoon of butter.

In a medium-sized saucepan, melt half of the remaining butter over moderate heat. Remove the pan from the heat and, with a wooden spoon, stir in the flour to make a smooth paste. Gradually add the milk, stirring constantly. Return the pan to the heat and cook, stirring constantly,

This fabulous Ice-Cream Roll is a guaranteed 'hit' at any children's party!

for 2 to 3 minutes, or until the mixture is thick and smooth. Add the nutmeg and 2 tablespoons of the sugar. Reduce the heat to low and simmer for 3 minutes. Remove the pan from the heat.

Pour the mixture into the baking dish and dot the surface with the remaining butter, cut into small pieces. Sprinkle the remaining sugar and the cinnamon thickly on top of the butter. Place the dish under the grill [broiler] and cook for 3 to 5 minutes or until the top is golden brown.

Serve hot or cold.

Ice-Cream Roll

Ideal to serve at a children's tea party or as a simple dessert, Ice-Cream Roll is cool and delicious. It may be decorated with glacé cherries and candied angelica before serving.

ONE ICE-CREAM ROLL

1 teaspoon vegetable oil
3 eggs
3 oz. [⅜ cup] castor sugar
3 oz. [¾ cup] flour, sifted
¼ teaspoon vanilla essence
1 tablespoon sifted cornflour [cornstarch]
FILLING
4 oz. strawberry jam

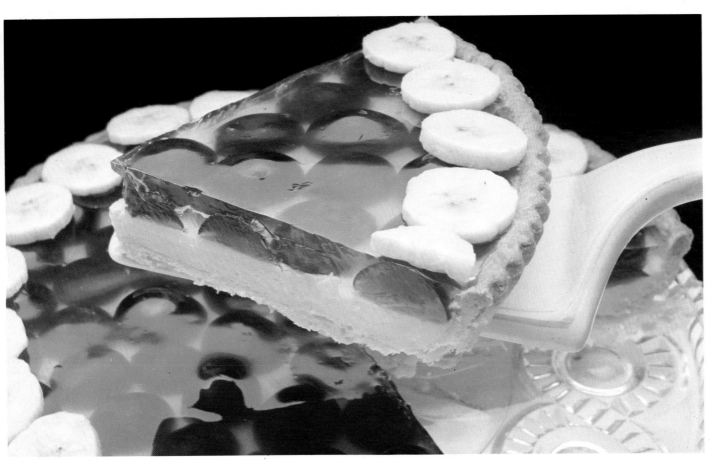

16 fl. oz. [2 cups] vanilla ice-cream

Preheat the oven to hot 425°F (Gas Mark 7, 220°C).

Line an 8- x 12-inch Swiss [jelly] roll tin with non-stick silicone paper or aluminium foil. If you use aluminium foil, grease it with the vegetable oil. Set the tin aside.

Put the eggs and sugar in a medium-sized heatproof mixing bowl. Place the bowl in a saucepan half-filled with hot water. Set the saucepan over moderately low heat.

Using a wire whisk or rotary beater, beat the eggs and sugar together until the mixture is very thick and will make a ribbon trail on itself when the whisk is lifted.

Remove the bowl from the saucepan. Using a metal spoon or spatula, fold in the flour and the vanilla essence.

Pour the batter into the prepared tin and smooth it down with a flat-bladed knife.

Place the tin in the centre of the oven and bake for 8 minutes, or until a skewer inserted into the centre of the sponge comes out clean.

Remove the tin from the oven.

Lay a piece of greaseproof or waxed paper flat on the working surface and dust it with the cornflour [cornstarch]. Turn the sponge out on to the paper. Carefully remove the silicone paper or

Pretty to look at, satisfying to eat Jelly Tart is the perfect—and economical—dessert for a family lunch or dinner.

foil from the sponge.

With a sharp knife, make a shallow cut across the sponge about 2½ inches from the end, to make the rolling easier. With the help of the greaseproof or waxed paper, carefully roll up the sponge, Swiss [jelly] roll style, with the paper inside. Set the cake aside to cool completely.

When the cake is cold, carefully unroll it. Discard the greaseproof or waxed paper and, using a flat-bladed knife, spread the jam evenly over the surface of the cake. Spread the ice-cream thickly on top of the jam.

Roll up the Swiss [jelly] roll and place it on a serving plate. Serve the roll immediately.

Jelly Tart

☆ ☆   ①   ⋈ ⋈ ⋈

This is not an easy dessert to make, since it requires great care in handling, but the final result is well worth the trouble! Any fruit in season may be used, but grapes, bananas and mandarin oranges are perhaps the most attractive. Serve for a family lunch or dinner with lots of stiffly whipped double

[heavy] *cream.*

4-6 SERVINGS

1 x 9-inch flan case, made with shortcrust pastry, baked blind and cooled
12 fl. oz. [1½ cups] thick custard
10 fl. oz. [1¼ cups] lemon jelly [gelatin], cool and on the point of setting
6 oz. black grapes, seeded, or 4 bananas, thinly sliced, or 4 mandarin oranges, separated into segments
1 banana, thinly sliced and sprinkled with 1 tablespoon lemon juice

Half-fill the flan case with the thick custard. Place the flan in the refrigerator and chill the custard for at least 30 minutes.

Remove the flan from the refrigerator and pour over half of the lemon jelly [gelatin]. Return the flan to the refrigerator for 30 minutes to allow the jelly [gelatin] to set.

When the jelly [gelatin] is set, cover it with a layer of fruit and pour over the remaining jelly [gelatin]. Place the flan in the refrigerator and leave until the jelly [gelatin] is completely set.

Remove the flan from the refrigerator. Place the banana slices decoratively around the edge of the flan case and serve at once.

Junket

This is the basic recipe for Junket. If you like, you can add 1 tablespoon of brandy to the milk just before you stir in the rennet. Or sprinkle grated nutmeg on top and serve with whipped cream.

4-6 SERVINGS

1 pint [2½ cups] milk
1 tablespoon sugar
1 teaspoon rennet

In a medium-sized saucepan, heat the milk and sugar to blood heat (98°F or 37°C) over moderate heat, stirring to dissolve the sugar.

Remove the pan from the heat and stir in the rennet. Pour the mixture into a serving dish and leave it to set at room temperature. Junket should not be put in the refrigerator.

Krammerhuse
GINGER CREAM-FILLED HORNS

Krammerhuse are Danish cones filled with whipped cream, served for a delicious dessert or afternoon tea. This variation of the basic recipe has the addition of ginger and Madeira to make it all the more superb.

38 CONES

3 oz. [⅜ cup] plus 4 teaspoons
    butter, melted
2 oz. [¼ cup] sugar
2 oz. [½ cup] flour, sifted
1 teaspoon ground ginger
4 large egg whites
8 fl. oz. double cream [1 cup heavy
    cream]
1 tablespoon Madeira
2 tablespoons chopped preserved
    ginger

Preheat the oven to fairly hot 400°F (Gas Mark 6, 200°C).

With 1 teaspoon of the butter, grease a large baking sheet. Set aside while you make the biscuit [cookie] mixture.

In a medium-sized bowl, combine 3 ounces [⅜ cup] of the remaining melted butter, the sugar, flour and ground ginger. Beat well with a wooden spoon to make a smooth paste.

In a medium-sized bowl, beat the egg whites with a wire whisk or rotary beater until they form stiff peaks.

With a metal spoon, carefully fold the egg whites into the batter.

Drop about eight teaspoonfuls of the

This elegant Lemon and Almond Flan is smooth and creamy to taste.

batter on to the baking sheet, leaving plenty of space between each spoonful. Gently flatten them with the spoon. Place the baking sheet in the oven and bake for 3 to 5 minutes or until the biscuits [cookies] are light golden.

Remove the baking sheet from the oven and loosen the biscuits [cookies] with a spatula. While they are still hot, form them quickly into cones by shaping them with your fingers.

Continue baking and shaping the biscuits, greasing the baking sheet with more melted butter when necessary. If the biscuits [cookies] become too cool and stiff to shape, return them to the oven for a few seconds to soften.

When all the biscuits [cookies] have been baked and shaped, allow them to cool.

In a small mixing bowl, beat the cream with a wire whisk or rotary beater until it is stiff. Stir in the Madeira and preserved ginger.

When the cones are completely cool, fill them with the cream and ginger mixture. Arrange the cones on a serving dish and serve.

Lemon and Almond Flan

Lemon and Almond Flan has a smooth and creamy filling thickly sprinkled with toasted almonds. It should be served cold with cream for lunch or dinner.

6-8 SERVINGS

1 x 9-inch flan case made from
    frozen and thawed shortcrust
    pastry, baked blind and cooled
FILLING
½ oz. gelatine
2 fl. oz. [¼ cup] hot water
3 egg yolks
4 oz. [½ cup] sugar
⅛ teaspoon salt
    finely grated rind of 1 lemon

6 fl. oz. [¾ cup] hot milk
½ teaspoon lemon essence
5 fl. oz. double cream [⅝ cup heavy
  cream]
3 egg whites
2 tablespoons slivered almonds,
  toasted

In a cup, soften the gelatine in the water. Place the cup in a pan of simmering water to dissolve the gelatine completely. Set aside.

In a medium-sized mixing bowl, beat the egg yolks, half the sugar, the salt and the lemon rind together with a wire whisk until they are pale and thick. Gradually add the hot milk, stirring constantly. Pour the mixture into a medium-sized saucepan and set it over low heat. Cook the custard gently, stirring constantly with a wooden spoon, for 6 to 8 minutes, or until it coats the back of the spoon. Be careful not to boil the custard or it will curdle.

Remove the pan from the heat and pour the custard through a strainer back into the bowl. Stir in the gelatine and the lemon essence. Allow the custard to cool to room temperature, then place it in the refrigerator to chill for about 45 minutes or until it is beginning to set.

Meanwhile, in a small mixing bowl, beat the cream with a wire whisk or rotary beater until it is thick but not stiff. Set aside.

In another bowl, beat the egg whites with a wire whisk or rotary beater until they are frothy. Add the remaining sugar and continue beating until they form stiff peaks.

With a metal spoon, fold the whipped cream into the almost setting custard. When it is completely mixed in, fold in the egg whites.

Pour the mixture into the pastry case. Place the flan in the refrigerator and chill —it for at least 2 hours, or until the filling is firm and very cold. Sprinkle over the toasted almonds and serve.

Lemon Bread Pudding

Easy and inexpensive to make, Lemon Bread Pudding is made with candied peel, almonds, lemon rind and white bread. Serve for a warming and filling winter or autumn dessert.

3-4 SERVINGS

1 teaspoon butter
6 large slices white bread, crusts
  removed and very generously
  buttered
2 tablespoons flaked blanched
  almonds
2 oz. [⅓ cup] chopped mixed
  candied peel
¼ teaspoon ground mixed spice or
  allspice
  finely grated rind of 2 lemons
2 tablespoons soft brown sugar
CUSTARD
2 eggs
¼ teaspoon vanilla essence
⅛ teaspoon almond essence
15 fl. oz. [1⅞ cups] milk
1 tablespoon sugar

Preheat the oven to fairly hot 375°F (Gas Mark 5, 190°C).

Using the teaspoon of butter, lightly grease a medium-sized shallow baking dish.

Cut the bread slices into quarters. Place a third of the bread quarters, buttered sides up, in the bottom of the prepared baking dish. Sprinkle over half the flaked almonds, candied peel, mixed spice or allspice, grated lemon rind and brown sugar.

Cover with a second layer of bread quarters. Sprinkle over the remaining almonds, candied peel, mixed spice or allspice, lemon rind and sugar. Cover with the remaining bread quarters, buttered sides up. Set aside.

To make the custard, beat the eggs, vanilla essence and almond essence together in a medium-sized mixing bowl. Set the bowl aside.

In a medium-sized saucepan, heat the milk and sugar over moderate heat. When the sugar has dissolved and the milk is hot, remove the pan from the heat. Beating constantly, gradually pour the hot milk into the beaten egg mixture.

Pour the custard through a fine wire strainer on to the bread layers in the dish. Set aside for 15 minutes, or until the bread has absorbed most of the liquid.

Place the dish in the centre of the oven and bake the pudding for 35 to 40 minutes, or until the top is golden and crisp.

Remove the pudding from the oven and serve immediately, straight from the dish.

Morello Cherries with Yogurt

A simple pudding with a very fresh flavour, Morello Cherries with Yogurt may be served for breakfast with cereal sprinkled on top, or as a simple lunch or dinner dessert for the family.

4 SERVINGS

1 lb. canned stoned Morello
   cherries, drained
3 oz. [½ cup] soft brown sugar
½ teaspoon ground ginger
½ teaspoon vanilla essence
15 fl. oz. [1⅞ cups] yogurt

In a large saucepan, heat the cherries and sugar over low heat, stirring frequently until the sugar has dissolved. Add the ginger and vanilla essence and stir well. Cover the pan and simmer the mixture for 5 to 8 minutes or until the cherries are very soft but not pulpy. Remove the pan from the heat.

Pour the cherry mixture into a heat-proof serving dish and allow to cool for 30 minutes. Then place the dish in the refrigerator to chill for 1 hour.

Remove the dish from the refrigerator and stir in the yogurt.

Serve immediately.

Pears Poached in Red Wine

Simple to make and absolutely delicious, Pears Poached in Red Wine may be served with whipped cream for a super family lunch or dinner.

6 SERVINGS

6 large firm pears
6 oz. [¾ cup] sugar
4 fl. oz. [½ cup] water
2-inch piece cinnamon stick
   pared rind of 1 lemon
4 fl. oz. [½ cup] red wine

With a sharp knife, peel the pears.

Place the pears, sugar, water, cinnamon stick and lemon rind in a large saucepan. Place the pan over moderate heat, cover and cook the pears for 10 minutes. Add the wine, reduce the heat to very low and simmer, turning occasionally, for a further 20 to 25 minutes or until the pears are tender but still firm when pierced with a sharp knife.

Using a slotted spoon, transfer the

This tempting Pineapple Upside-down Cake was originally American but is now a popular dessert cake all over the world.

pears to a serving dish and set aside.

Increase the heat to high and boil the cooking liquid for 8 minutes or until it has thickened slightly.

Remove the pan from the heat and strain the liquid over the pears. Set the dish aside at room temperature until the pears are cool, then chill them in the refrigerator for at least 1 to 1½ hours before serving.

Peach Flan

Sweet and melting Peach Flan is best made when fresh peaches are plentiful and cheap. Serve the flan with single [light] cream or, if you like really sweet desserts, brandy butter.

4-6 SERVINGS

1 x 9-inch flan case made with
   frozen and thawed shortcrust
   pastry, baked blind and cooled
4 large peaches, blanched, peeled,
   stoned and sliced
1 tablespoon peach brandy
   (optional)
TOPPING
2 tablespoons ground almonds
1 tablespoon chopped blanched
   almonds
1 tablespoon finely chopped
   walnuts
3 tablespoons soft brown sugar
1 teaspoon finely grated orange
   rind
1 tablespoon butter, cut into small
   pieces

Place the flan case on a flameproof serving dish. Arrange the peach slices in the flan case. Sprinkle over the peach brandy, if you are using it. Set the flan case aside.

Preheat the grill [broiler] to high.

To make the topping, in a small mixing bowl, combine the ground and chopped almonds, the walnuts, sugar and orange rind.

Sprinkle the topping over the peach slices and dot the top with the butter pieces.

Place the dish under the grill [broiler] and grill [broil] for 4 minutes or until the topping is crisp and bubbling.

Remove the dish from under the grill [broiler] and serve immediately, straight from the dish, or allow to cool completely before serving.

Pineapple Upside-down Cake

This is a well-known American cake in

which the fruit is arranged decoratively on the bottom of the cake tin and the batter is poured over the top. When the cake is baked it is turned out, upside-down, to display the fruit. Serve it with whipped cream or lots of cold, thick custard for a scrumptious family dessert. Or serve as a rich after-school snack.

9 SERVINGS

5 oz. [⅝ cup] plus 1 teaspoon
   butter, softened
2 tablespoons soft brown sugar
1 medium-sized fresh pineapple,
   peeled, cored and cut into 9 rings
   or 14 oz. canned pineapple rings,
   drained
9 glacé cherries
4 oz. [½ cup] sugar
2 eggs
6 oz. [1½ cups] self-raising flour,
   sifted
3 tablespoons milk
1-inch piece angelica cut into 18
   leaves (optional)

Preheat the oven to moderate 350°F (Gas Mark 4, 180°C).

With the teaspoon of the butter, lightly grease the sides of an 8- x 8-inch cake tin. Cut 1 ounce [2 tablespoons] of the remaining butter into small pieces and dot them over the base of the tin. Sprinkle the brown sugar carefully over the top. Arrange the pineapple slices decoratively on top of the sugar, and place a glacé cherry in the centre of each ring. Set the cake tin aside.

In a medium-sized mixing bowl, beat the remaining butter with a wooden spoon until it is soft and creamy. Add the sugar and cream it with the butter until the mixture is light and fluffy. Add the eggs, one at a time, beating well until they are thoroughly blended. Using a large metal spoon, fold in the flour. Stir in enough of the milk to give the batter a dropping consistency.

Spoon the batter into the cake tin, being careful not to dislodge the glacé cherries. Smooth down the top of the batter with a flat-bladed knife. Place the cake tin in the centre of the oven and bake the cake for 50 minutes to 1 hour or until the cake is golden brown and a skewer inserted into the centre of the cake comes out clean.

Remove the tin from the oven and allow the cake to cool for 5 minutes. Run a knife around the sides of the cake. Invert a serving dish over the cake tin and reverse the two. The cake should slide out easily. Decorate each cherry with two angelica leaves, if desired.

Serve the cake immediately or set it aside to cool completely before serving, cut into small portions.

Plum Compôte

Plum Compôte is a simple but delicious dessert which may be served cold, with whipped cream.

4 SERVINGS

10 fl. oz. [1¼ cups] water
6 oz. [¾ cup] sugar
   finely grated rind of ½ lemon
1½ lb. plums, halved and stoned

In a medium-sized saucepan, combine the water, sugar and lemon rind together. Set the pan over low heat and cook the mixture, stirring occasionally, until the sugar has dissolved. Increase the heat to moderate and boil the syrup for 5 minutes, without stirring, or until it has reduced and thickened slightly.

Add the plums to the pan, reduce the heat to low and simmer, stirring occasionally, for 3 to 5 minutes or until the plums are cooked but still retain their shape.

Remove the pan from the heat and set the compote aside for 30 minutes. Turn the compôte into a serving dish and set aside to cool completely or chill in the refrigerator before serving.

Prune and Apple Meringue Flan

A delicious combination of prunes, apples and meringue makes this pie an ideal dessert.

6-8 SERVINGS

1 x 9-inch flan case made with
   shortcrust pastry, uncooked
FILLING
6 oz. prunes, soaked overnight,
   drained, stoned and halved
8 oz. cooking apples, weighed after
   peeling, coring and slicing
1 teaspoon lemon juice
2 oz. [⅓ cup] sultanas or seedless
   raisins
½ teaspoon ground cinnamon
2 tablespoons sugar
MERINGUE
3 egg whites
6 oz. [¾ cup] castor sugar

Preheat the oven to fairly hot 400°F (Gas Mark 6, 200°C).

Place the flan case on a baking sheet.

In a medium-sized mixing bowl, combine the prunes, apples, lemon juice, sultanas or seedless raisins, cinnamon and 1 tablespoon of the sugar. Transfer the mixture to the flan case, smoothing it out evenly with a knife. Sprinkle over the remaining sugar. Place the sheet in the oven and bake the flan for 15 minutes.

Meanwhile, in a large mixing bowl, beat the egg whites with a wire whisk or rotary beater until they form stiff peaks. Beat in 1 tablespoon of the castor sugar and continue beating until the meringue is stiff and glossy. With a metal spoon, fold in the remaining sugar.

Remove the baking sheet from the oven. Reduce the oven temperature to moderate 350°F (Gas Mark 4, 180°C).

Spoon the meringue over the filling to cover it completely. Pull the meringue, using the back of the spoon, into decorative peaks.

Return the flan to the oven and continue baking for 20 to 25 minutes or until the meringue has set and is golden brown.

Remove the baking sheet from the oven. Transfer the flan to a serving dish and serve immediately.

Queen of Puddings

A traditional British pudding, Queen of Puddings is delicious and filling and is sure to be a great favourite with all the family.

4 SERVINGS

2 oz. [¼ cup] plus 1 teaspoon butter,
   softened
2 oz. [¼ cup] sugar
   finely grated rind of 2 lemons

4 oz. [2 cups] fresh white
   breadcrumbs
1 pint [2½ cups] milk
2 eggs, separated
3 tablespoons strawberry jam
4 oz. [½ cup] castor sugar

Preheat the oven to moderate 350°F (Gas Mark 4, 180°C).

Using the teaspoon of butter, grease an ovenproof dish and set aside.

Place the remaining butter, the sugar and lemon rind in a medium-sized mixing bowl. Beat well with a wooden spoon until the mixture is smooth and creamy. Stir in the breadcrumbs. In a small saucepan,

scald the milk over moderate heat. Pour the milk over the breadcrumb mixture in the bowl, stirring constantly with the wooden spoon. Set aside and leave to cool for 10 minutes.

With the spoon, beat the egg yolks into the mixture, one at a time. Pour the mixture into the prepared dish and place the dish in the oven. Bake for 35 to 45 minutes or until the pudding is firm to the touch. Remove the dish from the oven and set aside to cool slightly. Spread the jam over the pudding and set aside.

Reduce the oven temperature to very cool 275°F (Gas Mark 1, 140°C).

In a medium-sized mixing bowl, beat the egg whites with a wire whisk or rotary beater until they form stiff peaks. Add 1 tablespoon of the castor sugar and continue beating until the mixture is stiff and glossy.

With a large metal spoon, fold in the remaining castor sugar. Using a spatula spread the meringue over the pudding.

Return the dish to the oven and continue baking for 20 to 25 minutes or until the meringue has set and is golden brown.

Remove the pudding from the oven and serve immediately.

Railway Pudding

A delicious sweet cherry pudding, Railway Pudding can be served with warmed custard sauce.

6 SERVINGS

4 oz. [½ cup] plus 3 teaspoons butter
4 oz. [½ cup] sugar
2 eggs
2 tablespoons double [heavy] cream
   grated rind of 1 small lemon
½ teaspoon vanilla essence
6 oz. [1½ cups] flour
1 teaspoon baking powder
8 oz. sweet red cherries, halved
   and stoned

Grease a 2-pint [1½-quart] pudding basin with 2 teaspoons of the butter. Set the basin aside.

In a medium-sized mixing bowl, cream 4 ounces [½ cup] of the butter with a wooden spoon until it is light and fluffy. Add the sugar and beat the mixture until it is smooth and creamy. Beat the eggs in one at a time. Stir in the cream, lemon rind and vanilla essence. Sift the flour and baking powder on to the creamed mixture

and, using a metal spoon, fold in until it is combined. Stir in the cherries.

Fill a large saucepan one-third full of water and bring it to the boil over high heat.

Meanwhile, spoon the pudding mixture into the basin, smoothing the top over. Cut out a circle of greaseproof or waxed paper 4-inches wider than the basin. Using the remaining teaspoon of butter, grease the paper circle. Cut out a circle of aluminium foil, the same size as the paper circle, and place the two circles together, the buttered side of the paper away from the foil. Holding them firmly together, make a 1-inch pleat across the centre. Place the circles, buttered side down, over the pudding basin. With a piece of string, securely tie the foil and paper circles around the rim of the basin.

Place the basin in the saucepan. Cover the pan, reduce the heat to moderately low and steam the pudding for 2 hours. Add more boiling water to the pan during cooking if necessary.

Remove the pan from the heat and lift the basin out of the pan. Remove and discard the paper and foil. Place a serving dish, inverted, over the pudding basin and reverse the two. The pudding should slide out easily.

Serve immediately.

Raspberry Sauce

This delicious sauce is an excellent accompaniment to sponge puddings, and adds that special something to vanilla ice-cream. For a more luxurious sauce, add 1 or 2 tablespoons of kirsch.

ABOUT 10 FLUID OUNCES [1¼ CUPS]

1 lb. fresh raspberries, washed and
   hulled
2 oz. [¼ cup] sugar
2 teaspoons lemon juice
1 teaspoon arrowroot dissolved in
   1 tablespoon water

Place the raspberries in a medium-sized bowl and sprinkle over half the sugar. Set aside for 2 hours.

Using the back of a wooden spoon, rub the raspberries and any liquid from the bowl through a fine strainer held over a medium-sized saucepan. Discard the pulp remaining in the strainer.

Add the remaining sugar and the lemon juice and place the saucepan over high heat. Bring the purée to the boil, reduce the heat to low and stir in the dissolved arrowroot. Simmer the sauce for 2 to 3 minutes or until it is smooth and thick.

Remove the pan from the heat and pour the sauce into a sauceboat.

A marvellous mixture of custard, strawberry jam and meringue— that's Queen of Puddings.

Rhubarb Brown Betty

A wholesome and scrumptious family dessert, Rhubarb Brown Betty is even more delicious when served with whipped cream.

4-6 SERVINGS

- 6 oz. [¾ cup] plus 1 tablespoon butter, melted
- 4 oz. [2 cups] fresh brown breadcrumbs
- 6 oz. crushed digestive biscuits [1½ cups crushed graham crackers]
- 4 oz. [⅔ cup] soft brown sugar
- 1 teaspoon ground cinnamon
- ¼ teaspoon grated nutmeg
  grated rind of 1 lemon
  grated rind of 1 orange
- 1½ lb. cooked rhubarb
- 4 oz. [⅔ cup] sultanas or seedless

raisins

Preheat the oven to fairly hot 375°F (Gas Mark 5, 190°C). Using the tablespoon of butter, generously grease a medium-sized ovenproof dish. Set aside.

In a large bowl, combine the breadcrumbs, biscuits [crackers], sugar, cinnamon, nutmeg, lemon and orange rind and the remaining melted butter.

Place one-third of the mixture on the bottom of the prepared dish, smoothing it down with the back of the spoon. Cover with half of the rhubarb and sprinkle over half of the sultanas or raisins. Continue

A sustaining dessert to delight the whole family—that's Rhubarb Cream Flan.

making layers in this way until all the ingredients are used up, ending with a layer of the breadcrumb mixture.

Place the dish in the oven and bake for 30 minutes or until the top is golden.

Remove the dish from the oven and serve immediately.

Rhubarb Cream Flan

Serve Rhubarb Cream Flan warm, with cream.

4-6 SERVINGS

- 8 oz. [2 cups] shortcrust pastry
- 3 tablespoons water
- 2 lb. fresh rhubarb, trimmed, washed and cut into ½-inch lengths
- 6 oz. [¾ cup] sugar

20

1 oz. [2 tablespoons] butter
1 oz. [¼ cup] flour
12 fl. oz. single cream [1½ cups light
cream]
¼ teaspoon vanilla essence
2 eggs, separated

Using a floured rolling pin, roll the dough out into a circle approximately ⅛-inch thick. Lift the dough on the rolling pin and lay it over an 8-inch cake tin with a removable base. Ease the dough into the tin. Trim the dough so that it comes halfway up the sides. Discard any leftover dough. Place the tin in the refrigerator.

In a large pan, combine the water, rhubarb and 4 ounces [½ cup] of the sugar. Set the pan over low heat and cook, stirring occasionally, for 25 minutes or until the rhubarb is tender. Remove the pan from the heat, pour off any excess liquid and set the rhubarb aside to cool.

Remove the tin from the refrigerator and spoon in the rhubarb. Set aside.

Preheat the oven to moderate 350°F (Gas Mark 4, 180°C).

In a medium-sized saucepan, melt the butter over moderate heat. Remove the pan from the heat and stir in the flour to make a smooth paste. Gradually add the cream, stirring constantly and being careful to avoid lumps. Stir in the remaining sugar and the vanilla essence.

Return the pan to the heat and cook the sauce, stirring constantly, until it is thick and the sugar has dissolved. Remove the pan from the heat, cool the sauce to lukewarm and then beat in the egg yolks.

In a small mixing bowl, beat the egg whites with a wire whisk or rotary beater until they form stiff peaks. Using a metal spoon, fold the egg whites into the sauce.

Spoon the sauce over the rhubarb in the tin and place the tin in the centre of the oven. Bake the flan for 45 to 50 minutes or until the top is deep golden.

Remove the flan from the oven and set it aside to cool for 10 minutes. Carefully lift the sides of the tin and slide the flan on to a serving plate. Serve immediately.

Roly-Poly

Roly-Poly is an old-fashioned English steamed pudding which can be made with any kind of jam. Serve with custard or plenty of cream.

4-6 SERVINGS

8 oz. [2 cups] flour
1 teaspoon salt
2 tablespoons sugar
2 teaspoons baking powder
3 oz. [⅜ cup] shredded suet
10 to 12 tablespoons water

6 oz. raspberry jam
1 tablespoon milk

Sift the flour, salt, sugar and baking powder into a large mixing bowl. Stir in the suet. Gradually add 6 tablespoons of water to the mixture and knead lightly until the dough is light and pliable. Add more water if necessary, spoonful by spoonful, if the dough is too stiff.

Roll out the dough to a rectangle ¼-inch thick. Spread the jam evenly over the surface, leaving a margin of about ¼-inch all around the edge. With a pastry brush, brush the edges with the milk.

Roll up the dough Swiss [jelly] roll style, pressing the edges together to secure them. Wrap the roll loosely in greased aluminium foil, making a pleat in the foil to allow for expansion.

Half-fill a large saucepan with water and place it over high heat. When the water comes to the boil, put in the pudding, reduce the heat to moderate and steam for 2½ hours, replenishing the water when necessary. Unwrap the pudding and serve.

Russian Blackberry Cream

This delicately flavoured blackberry jelly [gelatin], topped with cream, makes a

refreshing dessert to end a dinner.

6 SERVINGS

2 lb. blackberries, hulled
2 fl. oz. [¼ cup] water
8 oz. [1 cup] sugar
1 oz. gelatine, dissolved in 4
tablespoons hot water
10 fl. oz. double cream [1¼ cups
heavy cream], whipped until thick
2 oz. [½ cup] flaked almonds

Put the blackberries, water and sugar in a saucepan. Bring the mixture to the boil, stirring constantly. Cover the pan and simmer over low heat for 20 minutes or until the blackberries are pulpy.

Remove the pan from the heat and pour the mixture into a strainer held over a bowl. Using the back of a wooden spoon, rub the berries through the strainer into the bowl. Stir in the dissolved gelatine.

Pour the mixture into a serving dish and set aside to cool, then chill in the refrigerator for 2 hours.

When the jelly [gelatin] has set, spread over the whipped cream and, using the back of a fork, make decorative swirls. Sprinkle over the almonds and serve.

Cool and refreshing to eat, Russian Blackberry Cream makes a perfect light summer dessert for the entire family.

Sago Pudding

Sago Pudding makes an excellent family dessert. Serve it either hot or cold accompanied by stewed fruit and whipped cream. Or stir in lots of strawberry jam.

2-3 SERVINGS

16 fl. oz. [2 cups] milk
2 oz. [⅓ cup] sago
½ teaspoon salt
1 tablespoon butter
2 oz. [¼ cup] sugar
½ teaspoon ground cinnamon
2 teaspoons grated lemon rind
2 egg yolks

Pour the milk into a medium-sized, heavy-based saucepan and set the pan over moderate heat. When the milk is hot but not boiling, sprinkle over the sago and salt. Bring the milk to the boil and cook, stirring constantly, for 10 minutes or until the mixture thickens and the sago becomes clear.

Meanwhile, preheat the oven to moderate 350°F (Gas Mark 4, 180°C). Grease a 3-pint [2-quart] soufflé or straight-sided ovenproof dish with the butter and set aside.

Reduce the heat to low and add the sugar, cinnamon and lemon rind to the saucepan containing the sago. Cook, stirring constantly, for 2 to 3 minutes or until the sugar dissolves. Remove the pan from the heat and stir in the egg yolks.

Pour the contents of the saucepan into the prepared dish and bake for 30 to 35 minutes or until the pudding is brown on top and of a thick creamy consistency. The pudding is now ready to serve if it is to be eaten hot.

Scandinavian Whipped Berry Pudding

Scandinavian Whipped Berry Pudding is simply delicious served with chilled whipped cream.

6 SERVINGS

1½ lb. canned raspberries
4 oz. [½ cup] castor sugar
2 oz. [½ cup] semolina
⅛ teaspoon almond essence

Pour the raspberries with the can juice into a medium-sized fine wire strainer

A delicious old-fashiond milk pudding, Sago Pudding makes a warming winter dessert.

held over a medium-sized mixing bowl. Using the back of a wooden spoon, rub the fruit through the strainer to form a purée. Discard the pips in the strainer. Alternatively, blend the fruit and juice in an electric blender.

Pour the fruit into a medium-sized saucepan and bring to the boil over moderate heat. Gradually add the sugar and the semolina, stirring constantly. Reduce the heat to low and simmer the mixture for 10 minutes, stirring occasionally.

Remove the pan from the heat and transfer the mixture to a large mixing bowl. Stir in the almond essence. Using a wire whisk or rotary beater, beat the mixture for 15 minutes or until it has doubled in volume and is light and fluffy.

Spoon the pudding into 6 individual serving dishes and serve immediately.

Soufflé Omelet

Soufflé Omelet is cooked in the oven rather than on the top of the stove — and the result is correspondingly different. Serve Soufflé Omelet plain or with whipped cream as an elegant dessert.

4-6 SERVINGS

1 teaspoon butter

1 tablespoon icing [confectioners']
   sugar
4 oz. [½ cup] sugar
6 egg yolks
1 tablespoon finely grated lemon
   rind
8 egg whites

Preheat the oven to hot 425°F (Gas Mark 7, 220°C). With the teaspoon of butter, lightly grease a 9- x 12-inch baking dish. Sprinkle over the icing [confectioners'] sugar, shaking out any excess. Set the dish aside.

In a large mixing bowl, beat the sugar, egg yolks and lemon rind together with a fork until the mixture is well mixed.

In another large mixing bowl, beat the egg whites with a wire whisk or rotary beater until they form stiff peaks. With a metal spoon, carefully fold the egg whites into the egg yolk mixture.

Pour the mixture into the prepared baking dish, shaping it into a dome shape with a flat-bladed knife. Place the dish in the oven and bake for 8 to 10 minutes or until the omelet is lightly browned.

Remove the dish from the oven and serve at once.

Strawberry Sponge Roll

A light, thin sponge filled with chopped fresh strawberries, Strawberry Sponge Roll makes a delicious dessert served on its own or with whipped cream or cold custard sauce.

4-6 SERVINGS

4 eggs
6 oz. [¾ cup] plus 6 tablespoons
   castor sugar
   finely grated rind of 1 large
   orange
1 lb. fresh strawberries, washed
   and hulled

Preheat the oven to fairly hot 400°F (Gas Mark 6, 200°C).

Line a 10- x 18-inch Swiss [jelly] roll tin with non-stick silicone paper or greaseproof or waxed paper and set the tin aside.

In a large mixing bowl, beat the eggs together with a wire whisk or rotary beater until they are well mixed. Add 6 ounces [¾ cup] of the castor sugar and the finely grated orange rind and continue beating until the mixture is fluffy.

Tasty Strawberry Sponge Roll.

Spoon the egg mixture into the prepared Swiss [jelly] roll tin and smooth it to the edges with the back of a metal spoon.

Place the tin in the centre of the oven and bake for 10 to 12 minutes or until the top of the sponge is golden brown and springs back when lightly pressed with a fingertip.

Meanwhile, chop half of the strawberries coarsely and place them in a medium-sized mixing bowl. Add 3 tablespoons of the remaining castor sugar and, using a metal spoon, stir well to mix.

Remove the tin from the oven. Spoon the chopped strawberries evenly over the sponge and, carefully lifting up one end of the silicone or greaseproof or waxed paper, carefully roll up the sponge Swiss [jelly] roll style.

Carefully transfer the roll to a large serving dish. Arrange the remaining whole strawberries over and around the roll and sprinkle over the remaining sugar. Set the roll aside to cool completely before serving.

Summer Pudding

This traditional British pudding does not require any cooking but it must be made the day before it is required. Summer Pudding is also good made with ripe blackberries or blackcurrants or a mixture of the two.

4-6 SERVINGS

1 teaspoon butter
2 lb. raspberries, hulled
4 oz. [½ cup] castor sugar
4 fl. oz. [½ cup] milk
8 slices stale white bread, crusts removed
10 fl. oz. double cream [1¼ cups heavy cream]

Using the teaspoon of butter, grease a deep pie dish or pudding basin.

Place the raspberries in a large mixing bowl and sprinkle over the sugar. Set aside. Using a teaspoon, sprinkle a little of the milk over each slice of bread to moisten it.

Line the dish or basin with two-thirds of the bread slices, overlapping the edges slightly. Pour the raspberries into the dish or basin and arrange the remaining bread slices on top to cover the raspberries.

Place a sheet of greaseproof or waxed

This traditional British Summer Pudding tastes even better than it looks!

paper on top of the dish or basin and put a plate, which is slightly smaller in diameter than the dish or basin, on top. Place a heavy weight on the plate and put the pudding in the refrigerator to chill for at least 8 hours or overnight.

Remove the pudding from the refrigerator and lift off the weight and the plate. Remove and discard the grease-proof or waxed paper. Invert a serving plate over the top of the dish or basin and, holding the two firmly together, reverse them giving a sharp shake. The pudding should slide out easily.

In a medium-sized serving bowl, using a wire whisk or rotary beater, beat the cream until it is thick but not stiff. Serve the pudding immediately, with the cream.

Swedish Custard Pie

A delicious pie, Swedish Custard Pie may be served hot or cold.

4-6 SERVINGS

8 oz. [1⅓ cups] soft brown sugar
8 oz. [1 cup] sugar
6 oz. [¾ cup] butter, melted
6 fl. oz. double cream [¾ cup heavy cream]
3 eggs
¾ teaspoon almond essence
1 x 9-inch flan case made with shortcrust pastry
1 teaspoon grated nutmeg

Preheat the oven to very hot 450°F (Gas Mark 8, 230°C).

Place the sugars, butter and cream in a medium-sized heatproof bowl and place the bowl over a medium-sized saucepan half-filled with boiling water. Set the pan over moderate heat. Cook the mixture, stirring constantly with a wooden spoon, until the sugar has dissolved and the mixture is thick enough to leave a ribbon trail on itself when the spoon is lifted.

Meanwhile, in a large mixing bowl, using a wire whisk or rotary beater, beat the eggs until they are pale and thick.

Remove the saucepan from the heat and the bowl from the saucepan. Gradually beat the sugar mixture into the eggs until they are thoroughly combined. Stir in the almond essence.

Place the flan case on a baking sheet and pour the filling into the flan case. Sprinkle over the nutmeg and place the baking sheet in the centre of the oven. Bake for 10 minutes.

Reduce the oven temperature to warm 325°F (Gas Mark 3, 170°C) and continue baking the pie for 30 minutes or until a skewer inserted into the centre of the filling comes out clean.

Remove the pie from the oven and carefully transfer it to a serving plate. Serve immediately, or allow to cool completely before serving.

Syllabub

A delightful dish that can be made in a moment, Syllabub is a traditional English dessert. Serve on its own or with poached fruit.

4-6 SERVINGS

2 oz. [¼ cup] sugar
   juice of 1 large lemon
   rind and juice of ½ orange
6 tablespoons medium-dry sherry
2 tablespoons brandy
10 fl. oz. double cream [1¼ cups heavy cream], beaten until thick

In a medium-sized mixing bowl, combine the sugar, lemon juice, orange rind and juice, sherry and brandy. Gradually pour the cream into the bowl, beating constantly with a kitchen fork until the ingredients are thoroughly combined.

Cover the bowl and chill it in the refrigerator for at least 30 minutes or until ready to serve.

Remove the bowl from the refrigerator and pour the syllabub into chilled individual serving dishes. Serve immediately.

Trifle

A marvellous concoction of cake, jelly [gelatin], fruit and custard, Trifle is a rich dessert to serve at dinner.

6 SERVINGS

1 x 7-inch stale sponge cake
2 fl. oz. [¼ cup] sweet sherry
12 fl. oz. [1½ cups] thick custard
15 oz. canned fruit cocktail, drained
12 fl. oz. [1½ cups] strawberry jelly [gelatin], cool and on the point of setting
10 fl. oz. double cream [1¼ cups heavy cream], stiffly whipped
4 oz. fresh strawberries, hulled, washed and halved
2 tablespoons slivered almonds

Break the sponge into small pieces and place it on the bottom of a large glass serving bowl. Pour over the sherry and set aside for 20 minutes. Stir in the custard and refrigerate for 30 minutes.

Stir the fruit cocktail into the jelly [gelatin] mixture, then pour it over the sponge mixture. Place the bowl in the refrigerator for 45 minutes to 1 hour or until the jelly [gelatin] has set.

Meanwhile, in a medium-sized mixing bowl, beat the cream with a wire whisk or rotary beater until it forms stiff peaks. Fold in half of the strawberries.

Spoon the cream mixture over the jelly [gelatin], decorate with the remaining strawberries and almonds and serve.

Swedish Custard Pie tastes equally delicious hot or cold.

Vanilla Soufflé

Vanilla Soufflé is quick and economical to make and may be served as a treat for the family or as a dinner party dessert.

6 SERVINGS

1½ oz. [3 tablespoons] **butter**
2 tablespoons icing [confectioners']
  sugar
8 fl. oz. [1 cup] milk
1 vanilla pod
1 oz. [¼ cup] flour
3 egg yolks
1 tablespoon sugar
5 egg whites

Preheat the oven to moderate 350°F (Gas Mark 4, 180°C). Using 1 tablespoon of the butter, grease a 2½-pint [1½-quart] soufflé dish. Sprinkle the bottom and sides of the dish with the icing [confectioners'] sugar, knocking out any excess.

Cool and refreshing, Watermelon and Banana Salad is a perfect summer dessert.

In a medium-sized saucepan, scald the milk and vanilla pod over moderate heat. Remove the pan from the heat, cover and set aside for 20 minutes. Remove the vanilla pod from the milk.

In a large saucepan, melt the remaining butter over moderate heat. Remove the pan from the heat and, with a wooden spoon, stir in the flour to make a smooth paste. Gradually add the hot milk, stirring constantly. Return the pan to the heat and cook the mixture, stirring constantly, for 2 minutes or until it is thick and smooth. Remove the pan from the heat and let the sauce cool slightly.

In a small mixing bowl, beat the egg yolks with the sugar and mix them into the cool sauce, a little at a time.

In a large mixing bowl, beat the egg whites with a wire whisk or rotary beater until they form stiff peaks.

With a metal spoon, carefully fold the egg whites into the sauce.

Spoon the mixture into the prepared soufflé dish. Place the dish in the oven and bake the soufflé for 20 to 30 minutes or until it is lightly browned on top and is well risen.

Remove the soufflé from the oven and serve at once.

Watermelon and Banana Salad

The exotic combination of watermelon, banana and rum gives Watermelon and Banana Salad a delightful contrast of colour, flavour and texture.

6 SERVINGS

1 large watermelon, cut in half
  lengthways
6 bananas, peeled and sliced
  juice of 1 lemon
  juice of 2 limes
4 fl. oz. [½ cup] white rum
2 oz. [¼ cup] plus 2 tablespoons
  sugar

Using a sharp knife, carefully scoop out the flesh of the watermelon and cut it into cubes, removing and discarding as many seeds as possible. Place the watermelon cubes in a medium-sized mixing bowl and gently combine them with the

26

banana slices. Set aside.

In a small bowl, combine the lemon and lime juice with the rum. Add the 2 ounces [¼ cup] of sugar and stir the mixture until the sugar has dissolved.

Spoon the watermelon and banana mixture into the melon halves and pour the rum mixture equally over the two halves. Place the melon in the refrigerator to chill for 30 minutes or until ready to serve.

Remove the melon from the refrigerator and place the halves on a serving dish. Sprinkle over the remaining 2 tablespoons of sugar and serve immediately.

Wheat and Fruit Dessert

A delicious dish from Israel, Wheat and Fruit Dessert may be served for dessert or breakfast. Almost any fruit purée may be substituted for the one suggested in this recipe.

6 SERVINGS

3 tablespoons wheat germ soaked for 1 hour in the juice of 2 oranges
4 medium-sized eating apples, cooked and pureed
4 tablespoons chopped walnuts
2 tablespoons slivered almonds
1 large orange, peeled, white pith removed and cut into segments grated rind of ½ orange
10 fl. oz. [1¼ cups] yogurt
2 tablespoons soft brown sugar

Put the soaked wheat germ into a large serving bowl. Mix in the apple purée, walnuts, almonds, orange segments and rind. Using a large metal spoon, stir gently to blend.

Place the bowl in the refrigerator to chill for 30 minutes. Spoon over the yogurt, sprinkle over the sugar and serve at once.

White Grape and Ginger Syllabub

An unusual and refreshing dessert, White Grape and Ginger Syllabub is the perfect dish to serve at dinner.

6 SERVINGS

2 lb. seedless white grapes, with 6 grapes reserved, halved
8 oz. crushed ginger biscuits

[2 cups crushed ginger cookies]
4 egg whites, stiffly beaten
8 oz. [1 cup] castor sugar
10 fl. oz. [1¼ cups] white wine juice of ½ lemon
15 fl. oz. double cream [1⅞ cups heavy cream]
4 oz. [1 cup] slivered almonds, toasted

Arrange one-quarter of the grapes on the bottom of a medium-sized serving bowl. Cover with one-quarter of the ginger biscuit [cookie] crumbs. Continue making layers in this way until the grapes and the ginger crumbs are used up. Set aside.

Place the beaten egg whites in a medium-sized mixing bowl. Beat in one-quarter of the sugar. Using a metal spoon, fold in the remaining sugar. Pour over the wine and lemon juice and stir the ingredients carefully until they are thoroughly combined. Set aside.

Pour the cream into a large mixing bowl and, using a wire whisk or rotary beater, beat the cream until it is thick but not stiff. Using a metal spoon, fold the egg white mixture into the cream. Pour the cream mixture over the fruit and biscuit [cookie] mixture and place in the refrigerator to chill for 2 hours.

Remove the bowl from the refrigerator.

Arrange the reserved grapes on top and sprinkle over the almonds. Serve.

White Peaches with Caramelized Sugar

White Peaches with Caramelized Sugar is a rich dessert which takes little time to prepare and tastes superb.

6 SERVINGS

6 white peaches, blanched, peeled, halved and stoned
3 fl. oz. [⅜ cup] brandy
1 pint double cream [2½ cups heavy cream], stiffly beaten
4 tablespoons soft brown sugar

Preheat the grill [broiler] to high.

Place the peaches in a flameproof serving dish. Sprinkle over the brandy and set aside for 10 minutes.

Using a flat-bladed knife, spread the cream over the peaches, making sure the surface is flat. Sprinkle over the sugar.

Place the dish under the grill [broiler]. Grill [broil] for 1 to 2 minutes or until the sugar has melted and formed a very dark brown crust.

Remove the dish from under the grill [broiler] and serve immediately.

Desserts for Special Occasions

Bananas Baked in Rum and Cream

A rich dessert, Bananas Baked with Rum and Cream is excellent for lunch or dinner.

4 SERVINGS

6 bananas
1 tablespoon castor sugar
6 tablespoons white rum
4 oz. [½ cup] crushed macaroons
4 tablespoons melted butter
10 fl. oz. double cream [1¼ cups
    heavy cream]

Preheat the oven to moderate 350°F (Gas Mark 4, 180°C).

Peel the bananas and put them in a greased baking dish. Sprinkle over the sugar and rum. Bake for 15 minutes.

Remove the dish from the oven and allow to cool for 10 minutes.

Reduce the oven to warm 325°F (Gas Mark 3, 170°C).

Mix the crushed macaroons with the melted butter. Pour the cream over the bananas. Sprinkle the macaroon mixture on top of the cream. Return the dish to the oven and bake for another 20 minutes. Serve hot, straight from the dish.

Bombe Coppelia

A rich and unusual dessert, Bombe Coppelia is a mouth-watering combination of coffee ice-cream and praline. To make this dessert you will require a large frozen food compartment in your refrigerator.

10-12 SERVINGS

3 pints [7½ cups] coffee-flavoured
    ice-cream, slightly softened in
    the refrigerator
8 egg yolks
4 oz. [½ cup] sugar
3 tablespoons dark rum
1 tablespoon water
10 fl. oz. double cream [1¼ cups
    heavy cream]
PRALINE
1 tablespoon vegetable oil
3 oz. [⅜ cup] castor sugar
3 oz. [½ cup] blanched almonds

Prepare a chilled 3-pint [2-quart] bombe mould by spooning a little of the ice-cream into the base. Working quickly, so that the ice-cream does not thaw too much, spoon scoops of the ice-cream into the mould and, with the back of a metal spoon, pat the ice-cream firmly against the sides. Press a chilled glass bowl, 1-inch smaller than the mould, inside the mould so that the ice-cream forms a solid wall between the bowl and the mould. Cut out

more slices of ice-cream to fill up any gaps in the walls.

Place the mould in the freezer and chill for 1 hour or until the ice-cream is completely firm. Chill the remaining ice-cream in a separate bowl for later use.

While the ice-cream is freezing, prepare the praline filling. Using a pastry brush, coat a baking sheet with the vegetable oil.

In a small saucepan, dissolve the castor sugar over very low heat. Add the almonds and cook, turning the nuts constantly, until they are browned. Remove the pan from the heat. Pour the mixture on to the greased baking sheet. Leave the mixture to cool for 10 minutes, or until it is firm.

Place the pieces of praline mixture between greaseproof or waxed paper. Pound them to a coarse powder with a wooden mallet or a rolling pin.

Set the praline aside while you prepare the bombe mixture. In a large bowl, beat the egg yolks with a wire whisk until they are pale and form a ribbon trail on themselves when the whisk is lifted.

Place the sugar, rum and water in a large saucepan and cook over moderate heat, stirring continuously with a wooden spoon. When the sugar has dissolved, bring the liquid to the boil. As soon as the syrup reaches a temperature of 230°F on a sugar thermometer, or a few drops of the syrup spooned into cold water immediately form a soft ball, remove the pan from the heat.

Slowly pour the hot syrup into the egg yolks, beating continuously with a wooden spoon. Continue to beat the mixture as it cools. Beat in the praline.

In a mixing bowl, beat the cream with a wire whisk until it forms stiff peaks. Gently fold the cream into the praline mixture. Continue folding until all the cream is blended.

Remove the ice-cream mould from the freezer and pour the praline mixture into the centre of the ice-cream shell. Return the mould to the freezer for 2 to 3 hours or until the praline is firm.

Remove the remaining ice-cream from the freezer, and allow to thaw for a few minutes, until it is soft enough to spread. With a rubber spatula, smooth the ice-cream slices over the praline filling and ice-cream shell in the mould. Cover the mould with foil. Return the bombe to the freezer for 8 hours or overnight.

Chill a serving plate for 15 minutes.

When you are ready to serve the bombe, unmould it by dipping the mould in hot water for about 30 seconds. Place the chilled plate upside-down on top of the mould. Pressing the plate down firmly on to the mould, turn the mould and plate over quickly. The bombe should slip out smoothly. Serve at once.

Chestnut Pudding

A subtle blend of chestnuts, chocolate and brandy makes this dessert (pictured on page 321) something really special. If at all possible use a good-quality Cognac rather than a cooking brandy for this recipe.

8-10 SERVINGS

1 teaspoon vegetable oil
2 lb. unsweetened chestnut purée
7 oz. [⅞ cup] unsalted butter
7 oz. [⅞ cup] sugar
10 oz. dark [semi-sweet] cooking
    chocolate, broken into small
    pieces
3 fl. oz. [⅜ cup] Cognac
DECORATION
10 fl. oz. double cream [1¼ cups
    heavy cream], whipped until
    stiff
6 oz. strawberries, hulled and
    washed

Using half the oil, grease a 2-pound loaf tin. Line the tin with a sheet of greaseproof or waxed paper and grease the paper with the remaining oil. Set the tin aside.

Using the back of a wooden spoon, rub the chestnut purée through a fine wire strainer into a medium-sized mixing bowl. Set aside.

In a large mixing bowl, cream the butter with a wooden spoon until it is smooth and creamy. Gradually add the sugar, beating constantly until the mixture is light and fluffy. Set the mixture aside.

In a small, heavy-based saucepan, melt the chocolate over low heat. Remove the pan from the heat and set aside to cool for 5 minutes.

Stir the chocolate and chestnut purée into the butter and sugar mixture. Pour in the Cognac. Beat the ingredients together until they are thoroughly combined.

Turn the mixture into the prepared tin and place the tin in the refrigerator to chill overnight.

To serve, remove the tin from the refrigerator and turn the mixture out on to a serving dish. Remove and discard the greaseproof or waxed paper.

Spoon the cream into a forcing bag fitted with ½-inch star-shaped nozzle. Pipe the cream over and around the chestnut mixture. Decorate the cream with the strawberries and serve the dessert at once.

Bombe Coppelia—cool, rich, elegant and delicious—the perfect special-occasion dessert.

Ginger Ale Fruit Jelly
[Gelatin]

Quick and easy to prepare, this attractive, refreshing fruit jelly [gelatin] is an ideal dessert for lunch. Canned oranges, cherries and apricots are better in this recipe as fresh ones may retard the setting process.

4 SERVINGS

½ oz. gelatine
2 tablespoons hot water
2 fl. oz. [¼ cup] boiling water
2 fl. oz. [¼ cup] lemon juice
8 fl. oz. [1 cup] ginger ale
1 tablespoon sugar
4 oz. canned mandarin oranges, drained
4 oz. canned morello cherries, drained
1 eating apple, cored and diced
1 banana, thinly sliced
6 oz. canned apricot halves, drained

Pretty and colourful, Ginger Ale Fruit Jelly [Gelatin] is a great family favourite!

In a small bowl, soften the gelatine in the hot water for 5 minutes.

Pour the boiling water into a medium-sized mixing bowl. Stir in the softened gelatine and continue stirring until the gelatine dissolves.

Stir in the lemon juice, ginger ale and sugar. Set the bowl aside for 1 hour, or until the jelly [gelatin] is just beginning to set.

Fold in the oranges, cherries, apple, banana and apricots. Pour the mixture into a 2-pint [1½-quart] mould and place it in the refrigerator.

Leave for 3 to 4 hours, or until the jelly [gelatin] is completely set.

Remove the mould from the refrigerator and dip the base quickly into hot water. Place a serving dish over the top

of the mould and reverse the two. Serve at once.

Norwegian Rhubarb Dessert

Deliciously cool and refreshing, Norwegian Rhubarb Dessert is an easy to prepare dessert for a summer dinner. The rhubarb should be young as it has a better colour and a sharper flavour.

6 SERVINGS

2 lb. rhubarb, washed and cut into 1-inch pieces
8 oz. [1 cup] sugar
2 fl. oz. [¼ cup] water
2 bananas, mashed
8 fl. oz. double cream [1 cup heavy cream]
2 egg whites

In a medium-sized saucepan, simmer the rhubarb, sugar and water over moderate heat, stirring occasionally, for 15 minutes, or until the rhubarb is soft.

Remove the pan from the heat. Drain the rhubarb and transfer it to a large mixing bowl. Discard the juice. Set the rhubarb aside to cool. When it is cool, stir in the mashed bananas and the double [heavy] cream.

In a small mixing bowl, beat the egg whites with a wire whisk or rotary beater until they form stiff peaks.

With a metal spoon, fold the egg whites into the rhubarb mixture. Spoon the mixture into a decorative medium-sized serving dish and place the dish in the refrigerator.

Leave to chill for at least 4 hours before serving.

Orange and Chocolate Mousse

This version of Orange and Chocolate Mousse is made with the zest of oranges, orange-flavoured liqueur, chocolate, cream and eggs. As the mousse is so rich, it should be served after a light meal.

4 SERVINGS

2 large firm, bright-skinned
  oranges
4 large sugar cubes
10 fl. oz. single cream [1¼ cups light
  cream]
1 small vanilla pod
4 egg yolks
6 oz. dark [semi-sweet] cooking
  chocolate, melted
2 tablespoons orange-flavoured
  liqueur
4 egg whites

Rub each orange all over with the sugar cubes to extract all the zest from the rind. Place the sugar in a small mixing bowl and crush the cubes with a wooden spoon. Set aside. Reserve the oranges for future use.

In a small saucepan, scald the cream (bring to just under boiling point) with the vanilla pod over moderate heat. Remove the pan from the heat. Remove the vanilla pod, wipe it dry and store it for future use.

Gradually add the hot cream to the sugar cubes, stirring constantly, and continue stirring until the sugar has completely dissolved. Set aside.

In a medium-sized heatproof mixing bowl, beat the egg yolks with a wire whisk or rotary beater until they are pale and frothy. Gradually beat in the sugar and cream mixture and combine them thoroughly.

Place the bowl in a large saucepan half-filled with hot water. Set the pan over low heat and cook the mixture, stirring constantly with a wooden spoon, for 5 to 6 minutes, or until it is thick enough to coat the spoon. Do not let the mixture boil or the eggs will scramble.

Remove the pan from the heat. Gradually beat in the melted chocolate. Stir in the orange-flavoured liqueur. Lift the bowl out of the pan and set it aside to cool completely.

In a medium-sized mixing bowl, beat the egg whites with a wire whisk or rotary beater until they form stiff peaks. With a metal spoon, carefully fold the beaten egg whites into the orange and chocolate mixture.

Spoon the mousse into a chilled glass serving dish and chill in the refrigerator for at least 2 hours before serving.

Peaches with Macaroon Cream Filling

A simple but rich dessert, Peaches with Macaroon Cream Filling may also be served in a pre-cooked flan case for lunch or dinner.

6 SERVINGS

6 peaches, blanched, peeled, halved
  and the stones removed
6 tablespoons redcurrant jelly
  dissolved in 1 tablespoon
  brandy
FILLING
10 fl. oz. [1¼ cups] milk
1 vanilla pod
2 eggs
2 egg yolks

2 oz. [¼ cup] sugar
1 tablespoon flour
1 oz. [2 tablespoons] unsalted butter
6 oz. [¾ cup] crushed macaroons
¼ teaspoon almond essence

First make the filling. In a medium-sized saucepan, scald the milk with the vanilla pod over moderate heat (bring to just below boiling point). Remove the pan from the heat. Set aside to cool slightly. Remove the vanilla pod, wipe it dry and store it for future use.

In a medium-sized mixing bowl, beat the eggs, egg yolks and sugar together with a wooden spoon until the mixture is pale and thick. Stir in the flour.

Gradually pour the cooled milk into the egg mixture, stirring constantly with the wooden spoon. Return the custard to the saucepan and bring to just under boiling point, stirring constantly.

Remove the pan from the heat and beat the thickened custard until it is smooth. Beat in the butter, crushed macaroons and almond essence. Spoon the custard mixture into a bowl and set aside to cool. When the mixture is cool, cover the bowl with aluminium foil and put it in the refrigerator for 30 minutes.

Place the peach halves in the refrigerator and chill them for 30 minutes.

Arrange the peach halves, cut sides up, on a chilled serving dish and spoon equal quantities of the filling into them. Pour equal amounts of the redcurrant jelly mixture over each filled peach.

Serve immediately.

Cooling Norwegian Rhubarb Dessert.

Pecan Pie

A delectable pie, one of the glories of American cuisine, Pecan Pie is so rich that it is best served in small wedges.

6-8 SERVINGS

1 x 9-inch flan case made with frozen and thawed shortcrust pastry
2 oz. [½ cup] whole pecans
3 eggs
8 fl. oz. golden syrup [1 cup light corn syrup]
3 oz. [½ cup] soft brown sugar
½ teaspoon vanilla essence
¼ teaspoon salt

Preheat the oven to fairly hot 375°F (Gas Mark 5, 190°C).

Place the flan case in the oven and bake blind for 10 minutes. Remove the flan case from the oven and remove the foil or paper and beans. Set aside for 10 minutes.

Increase the oven temperature to hot 425°F (Gas Mark 7, 220°C).

When the flan case has cooled, arrange the pecans, in concentric circles, on the bottom. Set aside.

In a medium-sized mixing bowl, beat the eggs with a wire whisk or rotary beater until they are light and frothy. Beat in the syrup, then the sugar, and continue beating until it has dissolved.

Add the vanilla essence and salt and beat the mixture until it is smooth.

Carefully pour the mixture into the flan case, taking care not to disturb the pecan circles — the pecans will rise to the top but will keep their pattern.

Place the pie in the oven and bake for 10 minutes. Reduce the oven temperature to moderate 350°F (Gas Mark 4, 180°C) and continue to bake the pie for a further 30 minutes.

Remove the pie from the oven and set it aside to cool completely before serving. As the pie cools, the filling will set and become firm.

Zabaglione

Sometimes called Coupe Siciliana, Zabaglione is a light egg and Marsala custard chilled until very cold and served in wine glasses.

4-6 SERVINGS

3 oz. [⅜ cup] sugar
2 fl. oz. [¼ cup] water
2 egg whites
6 egg yolks
3 tablespoons Marsala

In a small saucepan, dissolve the sugar in the water over low heat, stirring constantly. When the sugar has dissolved,

increase the heat to high and boil the syrup until the temperature registers 240°F on a sugar thermometer or until a little of the syrup dropped into cold water forms a soft ball. Remove the pan from the heat.

In a medium-sized mixing bowl, quickly whisk the egg whites with a wire whisk or rotary beater until they form stiff peaks. Pour on the syrup and continue whisking until the egg whites and syrup are well mixed. Set the mixing bowl aside.

In a medium-sized heatproof mixing bowl, combine the egg yolks with the Marsala. Place the bowl over a saucepan of barely simmering water.

Beat the egg yolks and Marsala with a wire whisk or rotary beater for 5 to 8 minutes or until the mixture is very thick and pale in colour.

When the mixture is thick, remove the bowl from the heat and fold the egg yolk mixture into the egg white mixture. Spoon the custard into wine glasses. Cover the glasses with plastic wrap and put them into the refrigerator to chill for at least 1 hour before serving.

This rich and filling Pecan Pie is traditionally served, in small wedges, at American Thanksgiving Day festivities.

Sweets and puddings for entertaining

Most people consider a spectacular finish essential to any special meal — especially when there are favoured guests around willing to be impressed! And it's with this in mind that the dishes included in this section have been selected; and they're show-stoppers every one, from the intriguing combination of cold ice-cream and hot meringue in Baked Alaska (page 354), through the cool elegance of Cherries with Marsala (page 355) and classic Diplomate Pudding (pictured above, page 359), to the most famous cake of them all the Viennese Sachertorte (page 372).

And we haven't forgotten those occasions when you have to impress on a strict budget, as a quick glance at (and some judicious testing from) the **For Budget Occasions** section will confirm — serve dishes like Apple Pudding (page 380) or Yeast Buckwheat Pancakes with Blackberries and Sour Cream (page 384) and you're sure to please.

While most of the recipes do take a bit of time to prepare, almost all of them can be made well in advance, even the day before — an invaluable help to even the most experienced hostess, especially since every one is absolutely guaranteed to more than repay any care and attention required to make it. Each and every one fulfills the criteria that desserts not only look absolutely fabulous but taste superb as well.

Apricot Condé

A classic French dessert, Apricot Condé makes an elegant end to a special dinner.

6 SERVINGS

- 1 teaspoon vegetable oil
- 4 oz. [⅔ cup] round-grain rice
- 1½ pints [3¾ cups] milk
- 12 oz. [1½ cups] sugar
- 1 oz. [2 tablespoons] butter
- ⅛ teaspoon salt
- 1 teaspoon vanilla essence
- 6 egg yolks, lightly beaten
- 2 lb. apricots, peeled and halved
- 8 fl. oz. [1 cup] water
- 2 tablespoons kirsch
- 1 oz. [¼ cup] flaked almonds

Preheat the oven to cool 300°F (Gas Mark 2, 150°C). Lightly grease an 8-inch soufflé dish with the oil. Set aside.

In a flameproof casserole, bring the rice, milk, 4 ounces [½ cup] of sugar, the butter, salt and vanilla essence to the boil over moderate heat, stirring constantly.

Cover the casserole and transfer it to the oven. Bake for 1 hour, or until all the liquid has been absorbed. Remove the casserole from the oven. Stir in the egg yolks and place the casserole over low heat. Cook, stirring constantly, for 3 minutes. Remove the casserole from the heat and set it aside to cool.

Slice half a pound of the apricots.

When the rice is cool, spoon one-third of it into the soufflé dish. Place half the apricot slices on top. Continue making layers, ending with the rice. Cover the dish and place it in the refrigerator to chill for 2 hours or until the rice is firm.

Meanwhile, in a saucepan, dissolve the remaining sugar in the water over moderate heat, stirring constantly. Add the remaining apricot halves. Reduce the heat to low and simmer for 10 minutes or until the apricots are tender but firm. Remove the pan from the heat.

With a slotted spoon, remove 12 apricot halves from the pan and set them aside. Purée the remaining halves with the syrup in a blender and return the purée to the saucepan. Return the pan to high heat. Boil for 3 minutes. Remove from the heat.

Stir in the kirsch and almonds. Set the sauce aside to cool. Then chill it in the refrigerator.

Unmould the pudding on to a serving dish. Arrange the reserved apricot halves on the top and around the sides. Spoon over the sauce and serve immediately.

Baked Alaska

An impressive dessert, Baked Alaska i

Baked Alaska is simply superb.

sponge cake topped with ice-cream and covered with meringue.

6 SERVINGS

1 tablespoon butter
3 oz. [¾ cup] plus 1 tablespoon flour
6 oz. [¾ cup] castor sugar
4 egg yolks, at room temperature
1 teaspoon vanilla essence
4 egg whites, at room temperature
1 teaspoon baking powder
¼ teaspoon salt
5 oz. apricot jam
2 pints [5 cups] vanilla ice-cream,
    softened

MERINGUE

6 egg whites
⅛ teaspoon salt
6 oz. [¾ cup] castor sugar

Preheat the oven to moderate 350°F (Gas Mark 4, 180°C). Grease two 8-inch sandwich tins with the butter.

Mix the 1 tablespoon of flour with 1 tablespoon of castor sugar and dust the sandwich tins with the mixture. Shake out any excess flour and sugar.

Put the egg yolks in a mixing bowl. Add the vanilla essence and beat with a wire whisk or rotary beater until the mixture is pale. Add the remaining sugar, reserving 4 tablespoons, and beat to mix.

In another mixing bowl beat the egg whites with a wire whisk or rotary beater until they form soft peaks. Add the reserved sugar and continue beating until the whites form stiff peaks.

Fold the beaten egg whites into the egg yolk mixture until they are mixed.

Sift the remaining flour with the baking powder and salt into the egg mixture.

Pour the mixture evenly into the two cake tins and bake in the oven for 25 minutes or until a skewer inserted into the cakes comes out clean. Turn the cakes out on to a rack to cool.

When the cakes have cooled, spread one cake with the apricot jam. Put the second cake on top. Trim off the corners to make an oval shape.

Put the ice-cream on a sheet of aluminium foil and mould it gently to the size of the cake. Cover with foil and place in the frozen food storage compartment of the refrigerator to become hard.

Preheat the oven to very hot 450°F (Gas Mark 8, 230°C).

In a medium-sized bowl, using a whisk or rotary beater, whip the egg whites and salt until they form stiff peaks. Add the sugar a little at a time and continue beating until the whites are glossy. Do not overbeat or the whites will begin to collapse.

Put the cake on a baking sheet. Remove the ice-cream from the refrigerator, take off the foil and place the ice-cream on top

of the cake. Cover the outside of the cake and the ice-cream with the meringue mixture, making sure there is no cake or ice-cream showing. (This must be done very quickly and the meringue must cover the ice-cream and cake completely or the ice-cream will melt.)

Put the baking sheet in the centre of the oven and bake it for 3 to 4 minutes, until the meringue turns a pale golden colour. Serve at once.

Cherries with Marsala

☆   ① ①   ╳ ╳

Cool and refreshing, Cherries with Marsala makes a luscious end to a rich meal.

4 SERVINGS

2 lb. canned stoned Morello
    cherries, drained
5 fl. oz. [⅝ cup] Marsala

Cool, refreshing and elegant — that's Cherries with Marsala.

1 tablespoon sugar
5 fl. oz. double cream [⅝ cup heavy
    cream], stiffly whipped

In a saucepan, bring the cherries, Marsala and sugar to the boil over moderate heat. Reduce the heat to low and simmer gently for 10 minutes.

Remove the pan from the heat. Transfer the cherries from the pan to a serving dish. Return the pan to the heat and boil the liquid for 3 to 4 minutes, or until it is thick and syrupy. Remove the pan from the heat and pour the syrup over the cherries.

Place the dish in the refrigerator and chill for at least 1 hour. Top the cherries with the whipped cream and serve.

35

Chestnut Dessert

This delectable French dessert of Madeira-soaked sponges, covered with chestnut purée and cream, is easy and quick to make. It makes a perfect dinner party dessert, as it can be made in advance.

4 SERVINGS

4 trifle sponge squares [4 small stale sponge cakes]
4 fl. oz. [½ cup] Madeira
8 oz. canned sweetened chestnut puree
5 fl. oz. double cream [⅝ cup heavy cream], stiffly whipped

Place the sponge cakes in four individual serving glasses, trimming them to fit the shape of the glass if necessary. Pour equal amounts of the Madeira over each sponge and set aside for 10 to 15 minutes, or until the sponges have absorbed all the Madeira.

Spoon the chestnut purée on top of the soaked sponges and smooth it down.

Fill a small forcing bag, fitted with a medium-sized star-shaped nozzle, with the whipped cream. Pipe the cream decoratively over the chestnut purée in the glasses.

Place the glasses in the refrigerator and chill the mixture for 30 to 40 minutes before serving.

Chocolate Chiffon Pie

A tempting American pie with a nutty pie crust and a chocolate cream filling, Chocolate Chiffon Pie will be a special treat for those people who love rich creamy desserts.

4-6 SERVINGS

PIE CRUST
5 oz. [1 cup] Brazil nuts
2 tablespoons sugar
FILLING
½ oz. gelatine
4 oz. [½ cup] sugar
¼ teaspoon salt
6 fl. oz. [¾ cup] milk
2 eggs, separated
6 oz. dark [semi-sweet] cooking chocolate, broken into pieces
1 teaspoon vanilla essence
6 fl. oz. double cream [¾ cup heavy cream], stiffly whipped
2 tablespoons chopped Brazil nuts

Preheat the oven to fairly hot 400°F (Gas Mark 6, 200°C).

To make the crust, grind the Brazil nuts either with a food mill or in an electric blender.

Put the ground nuts in a medium-sized bowl with the sugar and blend them together thoroughly, using the back of a spoon. If you prefer, the sugar may be blended into the nuts in the blender.

With your fingers, press the mixture into the bottom and around the sides of a 9-inch pie dish.

Place the dish in the oven and bake for 8 to 10 minutes, or until the crust is lightly browned. Remove the dish from the oven and leave to cool.

To make the filling, put the gelatine, half the sugar and the salt in the top part of a double saucepan or in a bowl placed over boiling water. With a wooden spoon, stir in the milk, egg yolks and chocolate.

Stirring constantly, cook for 6 minutes or until the gelatine has dissolved and the chocolate has melted. Remove the pan or bowl from the heat and beat the mixture until it is thoroughly blended. Stir in the vanilla essence and set aside to cool. Place in the refrigerator to chill for about 45 minutes.

Remove the chocolate mixture from the refrigerator. It should be just on the point of setting. With a metal spoon, fold 4 fluid ounces [½ cup] of the whipped cream into the chocolate mixture.

With a rotary beater or wire whisk, beat the egg whites until they are almost stiff. Add 2 teaspoons of the remaining sugar and continue to beat until the egg whites form stiff peaks. Using a metal spoon, fold the remaining sugar into the egg whites. Carefully fold the beaten egg whites into the chilled chocolate mixture. Pour the filling into the pie shell and place it in the refrigerator to chill for 3 hours or until it is firm. Decorate with the remaining whipped cream and the chopped Brazil nuts just before serving the pie.

Coupe Jacques

This classic French dessert is made of lemon and raspberry sorbet, served in individual shallow glass bowls, and moulded so that each half of the bowl is a different colour. The ice is topped with fresh fruit, steeped in kirsch, and decorated with blanched almonds. Any fruits suitable for fresh fruit salad may be used.

6 SERVINGS

1 pint assorted fresh fruit, cut into small pieces
2 tablespoons castor sugar
2 teaspoons lemon juice
7 tablespoons kirsch
1 pint [2½ cups] raspberry sorbet
1 pint [2½ cups] lemon sorbet

2 oz. [½ cup] blanched almonds, halved

In a medium-sized bowl, combine the fruit, sugar, lemon juice and 6 tablespoons of kirsch. Toss and mix the fruit well with a spoon. Cover the bowl and chill in the refrigerator for 1 hour.

Rinse 6 shallow glass bowls in cold water.

Put a large tablespoonful of raspberry sorbet and another of lemon sorbet side by side in each bowl, leaving a small space between the two sorbets.

Remove the fruit from the refrigerator and put a large tablespoonful of fruit on top and in between the two sorbets.

Sprinkle the Coupe Jacques with the remaining kirsch and decorate with blanched almonds. Serve the Coupe immediately.

Crème Brulee

GLAZED BAKED CUSTARD

A rich, delicious dessert, with a topping of crisp caramelized brown sugar, Creme Brulée makes an impressive end to a dinner party.

4 SERVINGS

2 oz. [¼ cup] castor sugar
5 egg yolks
16 fl. oz. double cream [2 cups heavy cream], scalded
1 teaspoon vanilla essence
2 oz. [⅓ cup] light brown sugar

In a large mixing bowl, beat the sugar and egg yolks with a wire whisk until they are pale and smooth, or until the mixture will form a ribbon trail on itself when the whisk is lifted. Gradually beat in the scalded cream.

Pour the mixture into a large, heavy saucepan. Place the pan over low heat and stir constantly with a wooden spoon until the crème is thick enough to coat the spoon. Do not allow the crème to boil. Remove the pan from the heat and beat the crème for 1 to 2 minutes. Stir in the vanilla essence.

Strain the creme into individual ramekins or a deep flameproof serving dish. Allow to cool and then place the crème in the refrigerator to chill for 2 hours.

Preheat the grill [broiler] to high.

Remove the ramekins or dish from the refrigerator and sprinkle the surface of the crème with a thick layer of light brown sugar. Place the dish on a baking sheet and put it under the grill [broiler]. Cook until the sugar melts and caramelizes, taking care to remove it before it burns. Serve at once.

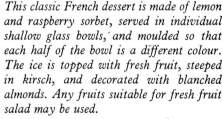

Small Custard Creams

This rich version of traditional small cups of custard is flavoured with coffee and brandy. Serve this filling dessert after a light main course.

6 SERVINGS

1 pint single cream [2½ cups light cream]
5 egg yolks
1 egg
3 tablespoons sugar
2 tablespoons coffee essence
2 tablespoons brandy

These rich Small Custard Creams are flavoured with coffee and brandy.

Preheat the oven to warm 325°F (Gas Mark 3, 170°C).

In a small saucepan, heat the cream over low heat. When the cream is hot but not boiling, remove the pan from the heat and set aside.

In a mixing bowl, beat the egg yolks, egg, sugar, coffee essence and brandy together with a wooden spoon until they are just combined. Stirring constantly with the spoon, gradually pour the cream on to the egg mixture, beating until they are well blended. Strain the mixture into another bowl.

Pour the mixture into 6 small ramekins or ovenproof custard cups. Place the filled dishes in a baking tin and pour in enough boiling water to come half way up the sides. Cover each dish with aluminium foil.

Place the tin in the oven and bake for 25 to 30 minutes or until the custards are lightly set.

Remove the tin from the oven and leave to cool, then chill in the refrigerator before serving.

Diplomate Pudding

This classic dessert (pictured on page 353) is rich with fruit soaked in kirsch. It may be served surrounded by fresh apricots.

6 SERVINGS

12 sponge finger biscuits [cookies], finely crushed
2 oz. [⅓ cup] sultanas or raisins
2 oz. [⅓ cup] raisins
4 fl. oz. [½ cup] kirsch
1 teaspoon vegetable oil
1¼ pints [3⅛ cups] milk
1 vanilla pod
5 tablespoons sugar
5 egg yolks
½ oz. gelatine, dissolved in 3 tablespoons boiling water
5 fl. oz. double cream [⅝ cup heavy cream]
4 glacé cherries, halved
4 fresh apricots, blanched, peeled, stoned and sliced

Place the sponge finger biscuit [cookie] crumbs, sultanas and raisins in a shallow dish. Pour over the kirsch. Leave the crumbs and fruit to soak for 1 hour.

Using a pastry brush, grease a 2½-pint [1½-quart] mould with the vegetable oil. Place the mould upside down on kitchen paper towels to drain off the excess oil.

In a medium-sized saucepan, warm the milk with the vanilla pod over moderate heat. When the milk is hot, but not boiling, remove it from the heat.

Put the sugar in a heatproof bowl. Make a well in the centre of the sugar. Drop the egg yolks, one at a time, into the well and, with a wooden spoon, beat the yolks, slowly incorporating the sugar. Continue this process until all the egg yolks and sugar are well mixed.

Remove the vanilla pod from the milk and, beating all the time, pour the milk on to the egg-and-sugar mixture.

Place a large pan, one-third full of water, over high heat. When the water is about to boil, reduce the heat to low. (The water must be hot, but not simmering.) Place the bowl in the water and, stirring slowly with the spoon, cook until the custard is thick enough to coat the spoon. Be careful not to overheat the custard as it will curdle. Remove the pan from the heat.

Stir the gelatine into the custard. Strain the custard into a large mixing bowl. Place the bowl over ice and stir until the custard thickens.

Two classic French cakes, fit to grace the finest table – Gâteau Noisette and Gâteau à l'Orange.

In a small bowl, whip the cream with a wire whisk until it is thick but not stiff. Lightly fold the cream into the thickening custard.

Cover the bottom of the mould with the cherries. Place the slices of apricot between the cherries, forming a wheel. Cover with a layer of one-quarter of the biscuit [cookie] mixture.

Pour one-quarter of the custard into the mould. Cover with another layer of the biscuit mixture. Repeat the layers until all the custard and biscuit mixture have been used up, finishing with a layer of the custard.

Cover the mould with foil and place in the refrigerator to chill for 6 hours, or until the pudding is completely set.

To serve, dip the bottom of the mould in hot water for 1 second. Run a knife around the edge of the pudding and turn it out on to a chilled serving dish.

Gâteau Noisette

Layers of meringue sandwiched together with a rich chocolate buttercream and covered with hazelnuts, Gâteau Noisette is a superb dessert for a dinner party.

8 SERVINGS

6 egg whites
12 oz. [1½ cups] castor sugar
FILLING
2 egg whites
4 oz. icing sugar [1 cup confectioners' sugar]
8 oz. [1 cup] unsalted butter
4 oz. dark [semi-sweet] cooking chocolate
1 teaspoon lemon juice
5 oz. [1 cup] chopped hazelnuts

Preheat the oven to cool 300°F (Gas Mark 2, 150°C). Line two large baking sheets with non-stick silicone paper.

In a mixing bowl, beat the egg whites with a wire whisk or rotary beater until they are light and frothy. Beat in 2 ounces [¼ cup] of the sugar and continue beating until the whites form stiff peaks. Carefully fold in the remaining sugar.

Spread the mixture into four circles, each about ¼-inch thick, two on each of the prepared baking sheets.

Place the baking sheets in the oven and bake for about 1 hour. Turn the circles over and bake for a further 15 minutes.

Remove the meringue circles from the oven and leave them to cool.

Meanwhile prepare the filling. In a mixing bowl set over a pan of simmering water, beat the egg whites with the icing [confectioners'] sugar until the mixture is thick. Remove the bowl from the heat.

In a second mixing bowl, cream the butter with a wooden spoon until it is fluffy. Beat in the egg white mixture.

In a small saucepan, melt the chocolate over low heat. As soon as it has melted, remove the pan from the heat.

Beat the melted chocolate into the egg white and butter mixture. Then beat in the lemon juice and half of the hazelnuts, beating until the mixture is well blended.

Carefully remove the meringue circles from the baking sheets.

Sandwich the circles together with the filling, covering the top as well.

Cover the top of the cake with the remaining hazelnuts. Leave the cake in a cool place for about a day before serving.

Gâteau a l'Orange

When Gâteau à l'Orange is to be served as a dessert, fill it with whipped cream and brush the sides and top with apricot glaze. Coat the sides with slivered almonds and decorate the top with glazed orange slices.

6-8 SERVINGS

1 teaspoon butter
4 oz. [1 cup] plus 1 tablespoon flour
4 eggs
4 oz. [½ cup] sugar
grated rind of 1 orange
4 tablespoons orange juice
4 oz. [½ cup] butter, melted

Preheat the oven to fairly hot 375°F (Gas Mark 5, 190°C). With the butter, grease a loose-bottomed 7-inch cake tin. Sprinkle in the tablespoon of flour and tip and rotate to distribute the flour evenly.

In a heatproof bowl, combine the eggs and sugar. Place the bowl in a pan of hot water, and put over low heat.

Whisk the eggs and sugar with a wire whisk or rotary beater until the mixture is light and pale and will make a ribbon trail on itself when the whisk is lifted. Remove the bowl from the heat and continue beating until the mixture is cool.

Using a metal spoon fold in the orange rind and juice.

Sift the remaining flour on to the surface of the egg mixture and gently fold it in. Pour the melted butter gradually into the mixture and fold and cut it in gently until it is all absorbed. Pour the mixture into the cake tin. Set the tin on a baking sheet and place it in the centre of the oven. Bake for 20 to 30 minutes, or until the cake will spring back when lightly pressed.

Remove the cake from the oven and allow it to cool for 5 minutes. Turn the cake out on to a wire rack to cool.

Serve cold, decorated as above.

Hazelnut Cream

Quick and easy to make, Hazelnut Cream is a delicious dinner party dessert of crushed hazelnuts and cream with a subtle flavouring of coffee. If you like, the cream may be decorated with a few hazelnuts just before serving.

4-6 SERVINGS

4 oz. [1 cup] whole hazelnuts, shelled and peeled
¼ oz. gelatine
2 tablespoons hot water
10 fl. oz. [1¼ cups] milk
4 egg yolks
4 oz. [½ cup] sugar
2 tablespoons coffee essence
10 fl. oz. double cream [1¼ cups heavy cream]

Using a blender or pestle and mortar, blend or pound the hazelnuts until they are coarsely crushed. Set the hazelnuts aside.

In a small saucepan, dissolve the gelatine in the water over low heat. Set aside.

In a medium-sized saucepan, bring the nuts and milk to the boil over moderately low heat, stirring constantly with a wooden spoon. Remove the pan from the heat.

In a medium-sized mixing bowl, beat the egg yolks and sugar together with a wire whisk or rotary beater until the mixture is pale and thick.

Pour the hot milk and nut mixture on to the egg yolk and sugar mixture, stirring constantly. Return the mixture to the saucepan and replace the saucepan over low heat.

Cook, stirring constantly, for 2 to 3 minutes, or until the mixture thickens and is smooth. Do not boil or the custard will curdle.

Remove the saucepan from the heat and stir in the dissolved gelatine and the coffee essence.

Pour the mixture into a medium-sized mixing bowl and set it aside to cool.

In another mixing bowl, beat the cream with a wire whisk or rotary beater until it is thick but not stiff.

When the hazelnut mixture is quite cold but not yet set, lightly but thoroughly fold in the beaten cream with a metal spoon.

Pour the mixture into a 2-pint [1½-quart] soufflé dish or bowl, or into individual dishes.

Cover the dish and place it in the refrigerator. Leave for at least 4 hours, or until the cream is completely set and firm.

Remove the dish from the refrigerator and serve at once.

Ile Flottante

FLOATING ISLAND

A classic French dessert, Ile Flottante is a rich mixture of kirsch and maraschino-soaked sponge cake 'floating' in a fresh fruit sauce. While a thin, creamy custard is often recommended rather than the raspberry or strawberry sauce suggested below, the latter is now a commonly accepted alternative. Serve after a light main course.

6-8 SERVINGS

1 x 8-inch round sponge cake, slightly stale
3 fl. oz. [⅜ cup] kirsch
3 fl. oz. [⅜ cup] maraschino liqueur
6 oz. apricot jam
2 tablespoons blanched slivered almonds
2 tablespoons chopped pistachio nuts
2 oz. [⅓ cup] raisins or currants, soaked in cold water for 2 hours and drained
10 fl. oz. double cream [1¼ cups heavy cream], very stiffly whipped
SAUCE
1 lb. fresh raspberries or hulled strawberries, washed
2 oz. [¼ cup] sugar
2 tablespoons lemon juice

With a sharp knife, slice the cake into four equal layers. Place the bottom layer in a large, wide serving dish and sprinkle it generously with about one-quarter of the kirsch and one-quarter of the maraschino liqueur. Spread the slice with about one-quarter of the apricot jam, then sprinkle on some almonds, pistachios and raisins or currants. Continue to make layers as above until all of the ingredients have been used up, reserving a few almonds, pistachios and raisins or currants for decoration. Place the dish in the refrigerator and chill for 15 minutes.

Remove the cake from the refrigerator and, using a flat-bladed knife, generously spread the top and sides with the beaten cream. Return the cake to the refrigerator to chill while you make the fruit sauce.

To make the sauce, rub the raspberries or strawberries through a fine strainer into a medium-sized mixing bowl, using the back of a wooden spoon to extract all the juices from the fruit. Discard the pulp remaining in the strainer. Alternatively, purée the fruit in an electric blender or in a food mill.

Stir the sugar and lemon juice into the fruit, beating with a fork until the mixture is well blended.

Remove the cake from the refrigerator

and spoon the sauce around it. Sprinkle the reserved almonds, pistachios and raisins or currants decoratively over the top.

Chill the mixture in the refrigerator for 15 minutes, then remove and serve cold.

Lemon Posset

A posset is an old-fashioned English dessert which, traditionally, would have been served in a china posset dish with a cover. The diarist Samuel Pepys' favourite

Ile Flottante is a sumptuous mixture of sponge cake, kirsch, maraschino, apricot jam and cream, 'floating' in a delightfully refreshing raspberry or strawberry sauce. Serve after a light main course.

posset was made with cream, sherry, egg yolks, sugar and spices and this version, although simpler, is equally rich, delicious and easy to make. Serve Lemon Posset with some sponge finger biscuits [cookies] or langues de chats.

4 SERVINGS

2 sugar cubes

1 lemon
10 fl. oz. double cream [1¼ cups heavy cream]
3 tablespoons dry white wine
2 tablespoons dry white vermouth
1 tablespoon sugar
2 egg whites

Rub the cubes of sugar over the surface of the lemon until they have absorbed all of the oil.

In a medium-sized mixing bowl, crush the sugar cubes using a wooden spoon or a fork. Using a wire whisk or rotary beater, beat in the cream. Continue

beating until the cream forms stiff peaks. Squeeze out the juice of half the lemon and carefully stir it into the cream with the wine and white vermouth. Stir in the sugar.

In another medium-sized mixing bowl, using a wire whisk or rotary beater, whisk the egg whites until they form stiff peaks. With a large metal spoon, carefully fold the beaten egg whites into the cream mixture.

Spoon the mixture into four individual serving glasses. Place the glasses in the refrigerator to chill for 1 hour.

Remove the dishes from the refrigerator and serve at once.

41

Macaroon and Apricot Whip

Macaroon and Apricot Whip is a delightful mixture of apricots, brown sugar, brandy, macaroons and ground almonds.

4-6 SERVINGS

8 oz. dried apricots, soaked overnight and drained
10 fl. oz. [1¼ cups] water
1 tablespoon lemon juice
2 tablespoons soft brown sugar
2 fl. oz. [¼ cup] brandy
16 macaroons, finely crushed
2 oz. [⅓ cup] ground almonds
1 teaspoon butter
4 egg whites

In a saucepan, bring the apricots and the water to the boil over moderate heat. Reduce the heat to low, cover the pan and simmer the apricots for 10 to 15 minutes or until they are tender. With a slotted spoon, lift out the apricots and put them in a blender. Blend at high speed until they are puréed.

Put the purée into a medium-sized mixing bowl. Stir in the lemon juice,

sugar, brandy, macaroons and almonds.

Preheat the oven to moderate 350°F (Gas Mark 4, 180°C). With the butter grease a 2-pint [1½-quart] baking dish.

In a large bowl, beat the egg whites with a wire whisk or rotary beater until they form stiff peaks.

Using a metal spoon, fold the egg whites into the apricot mixture. Pour the mixture into the baking dish. Put the dish in a deep baking tin. Pour in enough boiling water to come half way up the side of the dish. Put the baking tin in the oven and bake for 25 to 30 minutes or until the top is lightly browned.

Remove the dish from the oven and set it aside to cool. When it is cool put the whip in the refrigerator to chill for 1 to 1½ hours before serving.

Marmalade Chocolate Cake

A sumptuous chocolate cake with a tangy flavour, Marmalade Chocolate Cake makes an ideal festive cake. The cake can be decorated with crystallized flowers —

This rich, moist Marmalade Chocolate Cake makes a superb dessert, or it may be served for tea.

roses, violets, etc. as in the picture.

6-8 SERVINGS

CAKE
6 oz. [¾ cup] plus 1 teaspoon butter
6 oz. dark [semi-sweet] chocolate, broken into small pieces
8 oz. [1 cup] castor sugar
3 tablespoons orange marmalade
5 eggs, separated
8 oz. [2 cups] flour, sifted
2 teaspoons baking powder
2 oz. [⅓ cup] ground almonds

FILLING
8 oz. dark [semi-sweet] chocolate, broken into small pieces
2 oz. [¼ cup] butter, cut into pieces
2 eggs, well beaten

ICING
4 oz. dark [semi-sweet] chocolate, broken into small pieces
4 oz. [½ cup] butter, softened
10 oz. icing sugar [2½ cups confectioners' sugar]

1 tablespoon strong black coffee

Preheat the oven to warm 325°F (Gas Mark 3, 170°C).

With the teaspoon of butter, grease a 9-inch round cake tin and set it aside.

In a small saucepan, melt the chocolate over low heat, stirring occasionally. As soon as the chocolate has melted, remove the pan from the heat and set it aside.

In a mixing bowl, cream the remaining butter with a wooden spoon until it is soft. Beat in the sugar and continue beating until the mixture is fluffy. Cream in the melted chocolate and the marmalade.

Beat the egg yolks into the mixture, one at a time, adding a tablespoon of the flour with each yolk. Fold in the remaining flour, the baking powder and the almonds, and combine the batter thoroughly.

In a large mixing bowl, beat the egg whites with a wire whisk or rotary beater until they form stiff peaks. With a metal spoon, fold the whites into the batter.

Turn the batter into the prepared cake tin, smoothing it out with a knife.

Place the tin in the oven and bake for 1¼ hours or until a skewer inserted into the centre of the cake comes out clean.

Remove the cake from the oven and set it aside to cool for 30 minutes. Turn the cake out of the tin on to a wire rack and set it aside to cool completely.

Meanwhile, make the filling. Place the chocolate pieces in a heatproof mixing bowl set in a pan half filled with hot water. Set the pan over low heat and cook, stirring occasionally, until the chocolate has melted. With a wooden spoon, beat in the butter, a few pieces at a time, beating until it is well blended.

Using a small wire whisk or rotary beater, beat in the eggs. Cook the mixture, beating constantly, for 5 minutes, never letting the water come to the boil or the eggs will scramble. The mixture should have the consistency of custard.

Remove the pan from the heat. Lift the bowl out of the pan. Place it in the refrigerator to cool completely, stirring occasionally to prevent lumps from forming as the mixture thickens.

To make the icing, in a small saucepan, melt the chocolate over low heat, stirring occasionally. As soon as the chocolate has melted, remove the pan from the heat and set it aside.

In a medium-sized mixing bowl, cream the butter with a wooden spoon until it is soft. Sift in half of the icing [confectioners'] sugar and cream the mixture thoroughly. Beat in the melted chocolate and the coffee. Sift in the remaining icing [confectioners'] sugar and beat the mixture until it is smooth and creamy. Set

aside in a cool place.

When the cake is completely cold, slice it into four equal layers.

Set the top of the cake aside and place the three remaining layers flat on a working surface.

Spoon equal amounts of the filling on to each of the three layers. Spread the filling evenly over the layers to the edges. Sandwich the layers together, placing the reserved layer on top.

With a flat-bladed knife, spread the icing over the top and sides of the cake, bringing it up into decorative peaks.

Place the cake on a serving plate and set it aside in a cool place for 1 hour before slicing and serving.

Nectarine Cream Mould

A delicately flavoured cream, nectarine and brandy mixture, Nectarine Cream Mould makes a refreshing dessert.

4 SERVINGS

2 teaspoons vegetable oil
6 medium-sized nectarines, peeled, stoned and finely chopped
⅛ teaspoon ground allspice
3 oz. icing sugar [¾ cup confectioners' sugar]
2 tablespoons brandy
½ oz. gelatine dissolved in 4 tablespoons hot water
10 fl. oz. double cream [1¼ cups heavy cream]

Grease a 2-pint [1½-quart] mould with the oil. Place the mould, upside down, on kitchen paper towels to drain.

In a mixing bowl, combine the nectarines, allspice, sugar, brandy and gelatine.

In a small mixing bowl, beat the cream with a wire whisk or rotary beater until it forms stiff peaks. Fold the cream into the fruit mixture. Spoon the mixture into the prepared mould. Place the mould in the refrigerator to chill for 2 hours or until the dessert has set and is firm.

To unmould the dessert, run a knife around the edge to loosen the sides. Place a serving plate, inverted, over the mould and reverse the two, giving a sharp shake. The cream should slide out easily.

Nectarine Cream Mould makes a spectacular ending to dinner.

honey and kirsch dressing, Oriental Fruit Salad may be served on its own or with cream.

6 SERVINGS

4 fl. oz. [½ cup] clear honey
3 fl. oz. [⅜ cup] kirsch
10 dried figs, stalks removed and coarsely chopped
20 dried dates, halved and stoned
2½ oz. [½ cup] whole unblanched hazelnuts
2½ oz. [½ cup] whole unblanched almonds
1 medium-sized musk melon (honeydew, cantaloup, ogen, etc.)

In a medium-sized shallow dish, combine the honey and kirsch. Add the figs, dates, hazelnuts and almonds. Stir well to coat the fruit and nuts with the liquid. Cover the dish and set aside to soak at room temperature for 4 hours, stirring occasionally.

Using a sharp knife, cut the melon in half. With a sharp-edged metal spoon, scoop out and discard the seeds. Peel the melon and discard the skin. Chop the flesh into cubes.

Stir the melon cubes into the fruit and nut mixture. Place the dish in the refrigerator and chill the fruit salad for at least 1 hour.

Remove the fruit salad from the refrigerator and stir well. Divide the fruit, nuts and liquid equally among 6 individual serving glasses and serve immediately.

Parisian Fruit Tart

Succulent fruit encased in a rich walnut pastry and topped with whipped cream and nuts, Parisian Fruit Tart is usually served cold. It makes an absolutely delicious dessert for a summer or autumn dinner party.

4-6 SERVINGS

PASTRY
10 oz. [2½ cups] flour
½ teaspoon salt
3 oz. [⅜ cup] butter, cut into walnut-sized pieces
2 oz. [¼ cup] vegetable fat
4 oz. [½ cup] plus 2 tablespoons castor sugar
1½ oz. [¼ cup] walnuts, finely chopped
2 egg yolks, lightly beaten
3 tablespoons iced water

Orange Soufflés

These piping hot, pretty Orange Soufflés may be served with cream for a very special dessert.

6 SERVINGS

6 large oranges
1 oz. [2 tablespoons] butter
1 oz. [¼ cup] flour
10 fl. oz. [1¼ cups] hot milk
grated rind and juice of 1 orange
4 egg yolks
2 tablespoons sugar
5 egg whites

Cut about a ½-inch slice from the top of each orange so that the flesh and membranes may be extracted easily with a teaspoon. Discard the flesh and membranes. Cut out six pieces of aluminium foil large enough to cover the orange shells.

Place each orange shell in the centre of an aluminium foil square and draw up the edges of the foil until the orange shells are completely enclosed. Trim the edges of the aluminium foil with scissors so that they are level with the edge of the shell. Place the covered orange shells in a shallow ovenproof dish. Set aside.

Preheat the oven to moderate 350°F (Gas Mark 4, 180°C).

In a large saucepan, melt the butter over moderate heat. Remove the pan from the heat and, with a wooden spoon, stir in the flour to make a smooth paste. Gradually add the hot milk, stirring constantly.

Return the pan to the heat and cook the mixture, stirring constantly, for 2 minutes or until it is thick and smooth. Mix in the grated orange rind and juice. Remove the pan from the heat and let the mixture cool slightly.

In a small mixing bowl, beat the egg yolks and sugar together with a fork. Gradually mix them into the hot orange mixture.

In a large mixing bowl, beat the egg whites with a wire whisk or rotary beater until they form stiff peaks.

With a metal spoon, carefully fold the egg whites into the orange mixture.

Spoon the mixture into the prepared orange shells in the dish. Place the dish in the oven and bake the soufflés for 15 to 20 minutes or until they are lightly browned on top and have risen ½-inch above the tops of the shells.

Remove the dish from the oven. Peel the aluminium foil off the orange shells and serve immediately.

Oriental Fruit Salad

An unusual fruit salad made with dried figs, dates, nuts and melon cubes with a

1 egg white, lightly beaten
FILLING
2 oz. [¼ cup] sugar
5 fl. oz. [⅝ cup] water
4 large peaches, apples or pears,
  peeled, halved and cored
5 fl. oz. double cream [⅝ cup heavy
  cream], stiffly whipped
2 tablespoons chopped walnuts

First make the pastry. Sift the flour and salt into a large mixing bowl. Add the butter and the vegetable fat and cut them into small pieces with a table knife. Rub the fats into the flour with your fingertips until the mixture resembles coarse bread-crumbs. Mix in 4 ounces [½ cup] of the sugar and the finely chopped walnuts.

Add the egg yolks with a spoonful of the water and mix it in with the knife. With your hands, mix and knead the dough until it is smooth. Add more water if the dough is too dry. Wrap the dough in greaseproof or waxed paper and place it in the refrigerator to chill for 30 minutes.

Meanwhile make the filling. In a medium-sized saucepan, dissolve the sugar in the water over low heat, stirring constantly. When the sugar has dissolved, increase the heat to high and boil the syrup for 4 minutes.

Add the fruit halves, reduce the heat to low and simmer the fruit halves for 10 to 15 minutes or until they are tender but still firm. Remove the pan from the heat. Set aside to cool.

Preheat the oven to fairly hot 375°F (Gas Mark 5, 190°C).

On a lightly floured board, roll out two-thirds of the dough into a circle large enough to line a 9-inch flan ring. Lift the dough on the rolling pin and lay it over the flan ring. Gently ease the dough into the ring. Trim off any excess.

With a slotted spoon, remove the fruit from the pan. Arrange the fruit halves in a circle and cut sides down, in the dough case. Dampen the edges of the dough.

On a lightly floured board, roll out the remaining dough into a circle large enough to fit over the top of the tart.

Rich walnut pastry enclosing fresh fruit, makes Parisian Fruit Tart a special treat.

Using a 3-inch pastry cutter, cut a hole in the centre of the dough circle. Discard the small circle of dough. Lift the dough on the rolling pin and lay it over the tart. Using your fingers, gently press the dough edges together. Trim off any excess dough.

With a pastry brush, brush the top of the dough with the egg white and dust with the remaining 2 tablespoons of castor sugar.

Place the tart in the top of the oven and bake for 30 to 35 minutes or until the pastry is firm to the touch.

Remove the tart from the oven and set it aside to cool completely. When it is cold, carefully remove the tart from the flan ring.

Spoon the whipped cream into the centre of the tart and sprinkle with the chopped walnuts. Serve at once.

Paskha

Easter is the main festival of the Russian Orthodox church, a time when families come together, when a great deal of food is consumed, when rejoicing is general. Paskha, a luscious dessert made from cream cheese, sour cream, almonds and fruit, is an integral part of the feasting. A special pyramid-shaped perforated mould, called a paskha mould, is traditionally used to make this dish, but a flower pot or colander with suitable perforations may be substituted.

6-8 SERVINGS

2 lb. cream cheese
4 oz. [½ cup] butter, softened
4 fl. oz. [½ cup] sour cream
4 oz. [½ cup] sugar
1 egg yolk
½ teaspoon vanilla essence
   grated rind of 1 lemon
3 tablespoons sultanas or seedless
   raisins
2 tablespoons raisins
2 tablespoons slivered almonds
1 tablespoon slivered almonds,
   toasted
1 tablespoon chopped glacé
   cherries

Place the cream cheese in a large wire strainer set over a small mixing bowl. Cover the cheese with a clean cloth and place a heavy weight on top. Leave the cheese to drain for at least 1½ hours.

Discard any liquid in the bowl. Transfer the cheese to a large bowl. With a wooden spoon, beat the butter into the cheese, a little at a time, and continue beating until the mixture is blended.

In a medium-sized mixing bowl, combine the sour cream, sugar and egg yolk with a fork or spoon, beating until the sugar has dissolved. Gradually add the sour cream mixture to the cream cheese mixture, beating constantly. Beat in the vanilla essence and grated lemon rind. Fold in the sultanas or seedless raisins, the raisins, almonds, toasted almonds and glacé cherries. Set aside.

Line a paskha mould, if you have one, or some similar perforated mould, with cheesecloth. Spoon in the cream cheese mixture and smooth the top with a knife. Cover the mould with a damp cloth and place a heavy weight on top. Place the mould, on a large plate, in the refrigerator to chill for 8 hours or overnight.

To serve, remove the weight and cloth from the mould. Place a serving dish,

Pears in Chocolate Sauce is inexpensive, easy to make—and even easier to eat!

inverted, over the mould and reverse the two, giving the mould a sharp shake. The dessert should slide out easily. Remove and discard the cheesecloth. The paskha is now ready to decorate and serve.

Peach and Blackberry Dessert

Serve this delicious Peach and Blackberry Dessert on its own or with whipped cream for a super dessert.

4 SERVINGS

6 oz. [¾ cup] sugar
10 fl. oz. [1¼ cups] water
4 large peaches, blanched, peeled,
   halved and stoned
8 oz. blackberries
2 tablespoons brandy
DECORATION
12 large blackberries

In a medium-sized saucepan, dissolve the sugar in the water over low heat, stirring constantly. When the sugar has dissolved, increase the heat to moderate and boil the syrup for 3 minutes, without stirring.

Add the peach halves to the pan, cut sides down, and poach them for 3 to 5 minutes, or until they are just tender.

Remove the pan from the heat. Using a slotted spoon, transfer the peach halves to 4 individual serving glasses, allowing 2 peach halves for each glass. Set aside.

Pour off all but 2 fluid ounces [¼ cup] of the poaching syrup from the pan. Stir the blackberries and brandy into the reserved syrup and return the pan to moderately low heat. Cook the blackberries, stirring constantly, for 5 minutes, or until they are beginning to pulp.

Remove the pan from the heat. Strain the mixture into a small mixing bowl. Using the back of a wooden spoon, rub the blackberries through the strainer into the bowl. Discard any dry pulp remaining in the strainer.

Spoon the blackberry purée over the peaches. Decorate each glass with three of the whole blackberries.

Place the glasses in the refrigerator and chill the dessert for 1 hour before serving.

Pears Baked with Cardamom

Pears baked in liqueur and cardamom, Pears Baked with Cardamom makes a light dessert after a rich main course.

4-6 SERVINGS

3 large pears, peeled, halved and
   cored
2 tablespoons soft brown sugar

4 fl. oz. [½ cup] orange-flavoured
   liqueur
2 teaspoons ground cardamom
8 fl. oz. double cream [1 cup heavy
   cream], stiffly whipped

Preheat the oven to moderate 350°F (Gas Mark 4, 180°C).

Cut the pears into slices. Arrange them in a shallow ovenproof dish and sprinkle over the sugar. Pour the liqueur over the top, then sprinkle over the cardamom.

Place the dish in the oven and bake for 40 minutes or until the pear slices are tender. Transfer the pear mixture to individual serving dishes and set aside to cool completely.

When the pears are cold, spoon equal amounts of the cream into each dish and serve at once.

Pears with Chocolate Sauce

This delicious dessert is easy to make, inexpensive and will make a spectacular dinner party dish.

6 SERVINGS

1½ pints [3¾ cups] water
6 oz. [¾ cup] castor sugar
2 vanilla pods
4 cloves
6 ripe dessert pears
CHOCOLATE SAUCE
12 oz. dark [semi-sweet] cooking
   chocolate, broken into pieces
6 tablespoons water
1½ oz. [3 tablespoons] butter
3 tablespoons double [heavy] cream

In a medium-sized saucepan, combine the water, sugar, vanilla pods and cloves. Place the pan over moderate heat and bring the water to the boil, stirring constantly until the sugar has dissolved. Boil rapidly for 1 minute.

Peel the pears, leaving the stalks on. Slice about ¼-inch from the larger ends so that they can stand upright.

Place the pears upright in the syrup, reduce the heat to low and poach them for 15 to 20 minutes or until they are tender but still firm. Remove the pears from the pan and place them on a serving dish. Set aside to cool completely.

Meanwhile, make the chocolate sauce. In a heatproof bowl, combine the chocolate and water. Place the bowl in a pan of simmering water over low heat and cook, stirring constantly, until the mixture is smooth. Gradually beat in the butter and cream.

Remove the pan from the heat and the bowl from the pan. Pour the sauce over the pears and serve at once.

Pineapple with Kirsch

This very simple dessert is an ideal light and refreshing end to a rich meal.

4 SERVINGS

1 medium-sized fresh pineapple, peeled, cored and thinly sliced into rings
1 tablespoon castor sugar
2 fl. oz. [¼ cup] kirsch

Lay the pineapple rings in a medium-sized, shallow serving dish. Sprinkle on the sugar and pour over the kirsch.

Place the dish in the refrigerator and marinate the pineapple for 3 hours, basting and turning the slices frequently.

Remove the dish from the refrigerator and serve immediately.

Pistachio Ice-Cream

Pistachio Ice-Cream may be served sprinkled with toasted almonds or pistachios. For this ice-cream, an ice-cream container equipped with paddles or a hand-propelled ice-cream churn is essential.

1 PINT [2½ CUPS]

8 fl. oz. single cream [1 cup light cream]
4 oz. [1 cup] pistachios, shelled, blanched and chopped
8 fl. oz. double cream [1 cup heavy cream]
½ teaspoon almond essence
3 egg yolks
2 oz. [¼ cup] sugar
3 fl. oz. [⅜ cup] water
3 egg whites, stiffly beaten

Place the single [light] cream and the nuts in an electric blender. Blend, on and off, for 30 seconds or until the nuts are puréed within the cream.

Spoon the mixture into a small saucepan and, using a wooden spoon, stir in the double [heavy] cream. Place the pan over low heat and cook until the mixture is hot. Remove the pan from the heat. Cover the pan and leave it to cool.

Pour the cream mixture into a small mixing bowl. Beat in the almond essence and set aside.

In a medium-sized mixing bowl, beat

Pineapple with Kirsch is light and refreshing, and takes about 5 minutes to prepare.

the egg yolks with a wire whisk or rotary beater until they are well blended.

In a small saucepan, dissolve the sugar in the water over low heat, stirring constantly. When the sugar has dissolved, increase the heat to moderate and boil the syrup until the temperature reaches 220°F on a sugar thermometer or until a little of the syrup spooned out of the pan and cooled, will form a short thread when drawn out between your index finger and thumb. Remove the pan from the heat and let the syrup stand for 1 minute.

Pour the syrup over the egg yolks, whisking constantly with a wire whisk or rotary beater. Continue whisking until the mixture is thick and fluffy. Mix in the cooled cream mixture. With a metal spoon, fold in the egg whites.

Pour the mixture into an ice-cream container equipped with paddles or into a hand-propelled ice-cream churn, and freeze. Serve as required.

Raspberry Charlotte

This impressive dessert takes a surprisingly short time to prepare. If fresh raspberries are not in season, frozen ones are equally

good to use.

8-10 SERVINGS

25-30 sponge finger biscuits [cookies]
 4 oz. [½ cup] castor sugar
 8 egg yolks
 ½ oz. gelatine, dissolved in 2
  tablespoons hot water
 1½ lb. fresh raspberries, hulled and
  washed
 1¼ pints double cream [3⅛ cups
  heavy cream], stiffly whipped

Line the sides of a 3-pint [2-quart] mould with dampened greaseproof or waxed paper. Place a row of sponge fingers upright all around the inside of the mould, with the curved sides against the side. Do not line the bottom of the mould with biscuits [cookies].

In a heatproof bowl, beat the sugar into the egg yolks with a wire whisk. Continue beating until the mixture is pale yellow and will form a ribbon trail on itself when the whisk is lifted.

Place the mixing bowl over a saucepan of just-simmering water and continue beating, over moderate heat, until the mixture is thick and hot.

Remove the mixing bowl from the heat and stand it in a basin of cold water. Add the dissolved gelatine. Continue to beat the mixture until it is cold. Place the bowl in the refrigerator and leave it to chill for at least 30 minutes.

Strain 1 pound of the berries into a small bowl and measure out 16 fluid ounces [2 cups] of purée. Place the purée in the refrigerator to chill.

With a metal spoon, fold the chilled berry purée into the chilled egg yolk mixture. Add 1 pint [2½ cups] of the cream and stir until well blended.

Pour the mixture into the lined mould and arrange the remaining sponge fingers over the top to cover completely. Trim off any protruding sponge fingers.

Cover the mould with greaseproof or waxed paper and refrigerate for at least 6 hours or overnight.

To unmould the charlotte, remove the paper from the top and run a knife around the edge of the mould. Place a serving dish over the mould and reverse the two, giving a sharp shake. The charlotte should slide out easily. Decorate with the remaining berries and cream.

Raspberry and Redcurrant Compôte

A refreshing way to end a meal, Raspberry and Redcurrant Compôte should be served with vanilla ice-cream or whipped cream.

4-6 SERVINGS

This beautifully elegant Raspberry and Redcurrant Compôte makes a delightful dinner party dessert.

 1 lb. redcurrants, trimmed
 8 oz. cooking plums, halved and
  stoned
 8 oz. canned stoned Morello
  cherries, drained
 1 lb. [2 cups] sugar
 6 fl. oz. [¾ cup] water
 1 lb. raspberries, hulled and washed
 2 tablespoons medium sherry

Place the redcurrants, plums, cherries and sugar in a large saucepan. Pour over the water. Place the pan over low heat and stir constantly until the sugar has dissolved. Increase the heat to moderately low and cook the fruit for 20 to 25 minutes, stirring frequently, or until the mixture is soft and pulpy. Stir in the raspberries and continue cooking for a further 5 minutes. Set aside to cool to room temperature.

Stir in the sherry and pour the compôte into a glass serving bowl. Place the bowl in the refrigerator to chill for at least 1 hour.

Remove the dish from the refrigerator and serve immediately.

Redcurrant Cheesecake

☆ ① ① ① ✕ ✕

Redcurrant Cheesecake is a delicious combination of tart redcurrants mixed with cream cheese on a crunchy biscuit [cracker] base. The cheesecake is not cooked and is therefore simple and quick to make.

6 SERVINGS

4 oz. [½ cup] plus 1 teaspoon butter, melted

8 oz. crushed digestive biscuits [2 cups crushed graham crackers]

1 teaspoon ground cinnamon

1 lb. cream cheese

2 oz. [¼ cup] castor sugar

4 fl. oz. single cream [½ cup light cream]

1¼ lb. redcurrants, trimmed

½ oz. gelatine, dissolved in 2 tablespoons hot water

15 fl. oz. double cream [1⅞ cups heavy cream]

1 egg white, stiffly beaten

This filling, delicious Redcurrant Cheesecake tastes even better than it looks!

Lightly grease a 9-inch loose-bottomed cake tin with the teaspoon of butter.

In a medium-sized mixing bowl, combine the crushed biscuits [crackers], the remaining melted butter and the cinnamon together with a wooden spoon. Line the base of the cake tin with the biscuit [cracker] mixture, pressing it firmly against the bottom of the tin with your fingers. Set aside.

In a medium-sized mixing bowl, beat the cream cheese and sugar together with the wooden spoon until the mixture is smooth and creamy. Stir in the single [light] cream and 1 pound of the redcurrants. Beat in the dissolved gelatine mixture and spoon the mixture on to the biscuit [cracker] base. Place the tin in the refrigerator to chill for 30 minutes or until

the mixture has set.

Meanwhile, in a large mixing bowl, beat the double [heavy] cream with a wire whisk or rotary beater until it forms stiff peaks. With a large metal spoon, fold the egg white into the cream.

Remove the cake tin from the refrigerator. Spoon the cream mixture on to the cheesecake, making swirling patterns with the back of the spoon.

Sprinkle the remaining redcurrants over the cream. Serve immediately, or return to the refrigerator until required.

Rhubarb and Ginger Compôte

☆ ① ① ① ✕

Rhubarb and Ginger Compôte illustrates how well gin complements the flavour of rhubarb. It makes an ideal dessert for a summer dinner party. Serve with cream.

4 SERVINGS

50

8 oz. [1 cup] sugar
4 fl. oz. [½ cup] water
2 lb. fresh rhubarb, trimmed,
   washed and chopped
8 fl. oz. [1 cup] gin
1 tablespoon finely grated orange
   rind
¼ teaspoon grated nutmeg
½ teaspoon ground ginger
1 tablespoon preserved ginger,
   finely chopped

In a large, heavy-based saucepan, dissolve the sugar in the water over low heat, stirring frequently. When the sugar has dissolved, increase the heat to moderately high and bring the syrup to the boil, without stirring.

Add the rhubarb, gin, orange rind, nutmeg and ground ginger to the pan and reduce the heat to low. Simmer the mixture for 25 minutes or until the rhubarb is tender. Using a slotted spoon, transfer the rhubarb to a serving dish.

Increase the heat to high and bring the cooking liquid to the boil. Boil for 10 to 12 minutes or until the liquid has reduced by about one-third. Remove the pan from the heat and pour the syrup over the rhubarb. Sprinkle the chopped ginger over the top and put the dish in the refrigerator to chill for at least 30 minutes.

Remove the dish from the refrigerator and serve immediately.

Russian Gooseberry Cream

An easy-to-make dessert, Russian Gooseberry Cream has a delicate creamy texture. Serve with langues de chats.

4 SERVINGS
1 lb. gooseberries, trimmed and
   washed
1 tablespoon dried elderflowers
   (optional)
10 fl. oz. [1¼ cups] water
4 fl. oz. [½ cup] dry white wine
   very finely grated rind of 1
   lemon
4 oz. [½ cup] sugar
3 eggs, separated

In a medium-sized saucepan, bring the goosebarries, elderflowers if you are using them, water, wine and lemon rind to the boil over moderate heat. Reduce the heat to low and simmer, stirring occasionally, for 20 minutes or until the gooseberries are soft.

Remove the pan from the heat. Using the back of a wooden spoon, rub the gooseberry mixture through a strainer into a bowl. Discard the pulp left in the

strainer. Rinse and thoroughly wipe dry the saucepan.

Return the purée to the saucepan. Add the sugar and place the pan over low heat. Using the wooden spoon, stir the purée mixture until the sugar has dissolved. Remove the pan from the heat.

Beat the egg yolks into the gooseberry mixture and set it aside to cool to lukewarm.

In a medium-sized mixing bowl, beat the egg whites with a wire whisk or rotary beater until they form stiff peaks. Set aside.

With a metal spoon, fold the egg whites into the gooseberry mixture. Pour the gooseberry mixture into a large glass serving bowl or individual serving dishes. Set aside in a cool place for 1 hour or until the cream has set. Either serve immediately or chill the cream in the refrigerator until required.

This unusual dessert combines gooseberries, elderflowers, wine, lemon, sugar and eggs, in a rich purée. Serve Russian Gooseberry Cream, after a light main course, with delicate langues de chats.

Sachertorte

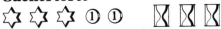

A rich moist chocolate cake, Sachertorte, the speciality of the elegant Sacher Hotel in Vienna, is almost the national cake of Austria. Sachertorte is traditionally served with lots of freshly whipped cream.

6-8 SERVINGS

4 oz. [½ cup] plus 1 teaspoon butter
6 oz. dark [semi-sweet] cooking chocolate, broken into pieces
6 oz. [¾ cup] sugar
1 teaspoon vanilla essence
6 egg yolks
3 oz. [¾ cup] flour
8 egg whites, stiffly whipped
6 tablespoons apricot jam

CHOCOLATE ICING
8 oz. dark [semi-sweet] cooking chocolate, broken into pieces
4 fl. oz. double cream [½ cup heavy cream]
12 oz. icing sugar [3 cups confectioners' sugar]

Preheat the oven to moderate 350°F (Gas Mark 4, 180°C). With the teaspoon of butter, grease a 9-inch cake tin with a removable base. Set aside.

In a heatproof bowl set over a pan of simmering water, melt the chocolate over low heat. Remove the pan from the heat and lift the bowl out of the pan. Set aside.

In a mixing bowl, beat the remaining butter and the sugar together until they are light and fluffy. Beat in the melted chocolate and the vanilla essence.

Gradually beat in the egg yolks, one at a time, adding a tablespoon of flour with each yolk. With a metal spoon, fold in the remaining flour, and then the egg whites. Spoon the batter into the prepared cake tin and smooth over the top with the back of the spoon. Place the tin in the centre of the oven. Bake for 50 minutes to 1 hour or until a skewer inserted into the centre of the cake comes out clean.

Remove the cake from the oven and set it aside to cool in the tin for 30 minutes.

The dessert to end all desserts—rich, elegant Sachertorte.

Turn the cake out of the tin on to a wire rack and slice it in half, crosswise. Set aside to cool completely.

Meanwhile, in a small saucepan, melt the apricot jam over low heat, stirring constantly. Remove from the heat and set the jam aside to cool to lukewarm.

Meanwhile, make the icing. In a heat-proof bowl set over a pan of simmering water, melt the chocolate over low heat. Remove the pan from the heat and lift the bowl out of the pan. Set aside to cool for 10 minutes. Beat in the cream and icing [confectioners'] sugar, beating until the mixture is smooth.

Using a flat-bladed knife, spread half the apricot glaze over the top of the bottom cake half and sandwich the two halves together. Spread the rest of the glaze over the top and sides of the cake.

Rinse the knife and spread the chocolate icing over the top and sides of the cake, ensuring that the icing is smooth.

Place the cake on a decorative serving plate and set aside in a cool place for 2 hours, or until the icing has set.

Sherry Jelly [Gelatin]

This simple-to-make dish may be made well in advance and, for the best flavour, removed from the refrigerator and unmoulded 30 minutes before serving.

4-6 SERVINGS

1½ oz. gelatine
4 fl. oz. [½ cup] cold water
8 fl. oz. [1 cup] boiling water
4 oz. [½ cup] sugar
¼ teaspoon salt
4 fl. oz. [½ cup] orange juice
2 tablespoons lemon juice
12 fl. oz. [1½ cups] medium sherry

Place the gelatine and cold water in a mixing bowl. Pour over the boiling water and stir until the gelatine has dissolved. Add the sugar and stir until it has dissolved. Stir in the salt. Set the gelatine mixture aside to cool for 10 minutes.

In a large jug, combine the orange juice, lemon juice and sherry. Pour the gelatine mixture into the jug, stirring constantly.

Rinse a 1½-pint [1-quart] mould in water. Pour the sherry mixture into the mould and chill in the refrigerator for 4 hours or until the jelly [gelatin] has set.

Remove the mould from the refrigerator. Pull the mixture away from the sides of the mould and quickly dip the bottom of the mould in hot water. Invert a chilled serving dish over the mould and reverse. The jelly [gelatin] should slide out easily. Serve immediately.

Sorbet with Apricots

Sorbet with Apricots is a light, refreshing dessert to serve after a rich main course.

4 SERVINGS

1 lb. canned apricot halves, drained and juice reserved
2 oz. [¼ cup] castor sugar
2 tablespoons fresh orange juice
2 tablespoons fresh lemon juice
2 egg whites, stiffly beaten
2 drops vanilla essence

Set the thermostat of the refrigerator to its coldest setting.

Put half the apricots in a blender and purée them at high speed. Pour the purée into a large measuring jug and repeat the process with the remaining apricots. Measure the purée and mix in enough of the reserved can juice to make 16 fluid ounces [2 cups].

Transfer the purée to a mixing bowl and stir in the sugar, orange and lemon juice. Using a wire whisk or rotary beater, whisk the egg whites into the

Smooth Sorbet with Apricots.

mixture until it is smooth. Stir in the vanilla essence. Pour the mixture into a freezer tray and place the tray in the frozen food storage compartment of the refrigerator. Freeze for 30 minutes or until the mixture has begun to set around the edges.

Remove the tray from the refrigerator and scrape the apricot mixture into a medium-sized mixing bowl. Using a wire whisk or rotary beater, beat the mixture until it is smooth. Return the mixture to the freezer tray and the tray to the frozen food storage compartment. Freeze for a further 4 hours or until the sorbet is firm.

Meanwhile, chill 4 individual serving glasses in the refrigerator for 30 minutes before you serve the sorbet.

Remove the glasses from the refrigerator and the freezer tray from the frozen food storage compartment. Using a tablespoon which has been dipped in hot water, spoon the sorbet into the chilled glasses. Serve immediately.

Strawberries Romanoff

This glorious dish makes a perfect dessert for a summer dinner party. Serve after a fairly filling main course.

4-6 SERVINGS

2 lb. fresh strawberries, hulled and washed
4 fl. oz. [½ cup] orange-flavoured liqueur
2 fl. oz. [¼ cup] fresh orange juice, strained

CREME CHANTILLY

10 fl. oz. double cream [1¼ cups heavy cream], chilled
1 teaspoon vanilla essence
1 teaspoon castor sugar

Place the strawberries in a deep bowl and pour the orange-flavoured liqueur and orange juice over them. Cover the bowl and place it in the refrigerator.

Leave the strawberries to chill for 2 hours, basting them occasionally with the liquid in the bowl. Transfer the strawberries and liquid to a serving dish.

To make the crème, in a chilled, medium-sized mixing bowl, beat the cream with a wire whisk or rotary beater until it forms soft peaks. Add the vanilla essence and sugar and beat until the mixture forms stiff peaks.

Fill a forcing bag with the crème chantilly and pipe it around the strawberries, or in decorative swirls over the top of them. Serve at once.

Strawberry Shortcake

A lovely dessert for a summer lunch or dinner, Strawberry Shortcake is an attractive way to serve strawberries.

4-8 SERVINGS

6 oz. [¾ cup] plus 1 teaspoon butter, softened
8 oz. [2 cups] flour
2 oz. icing sugar [½ cup confectioners' sugar]
1 egg yolk
10 fl. oz. double cream [1¼ cups heavy cream]
1 lb. strawberries, hulled and washed
2 tablespoons castor sugar

Using the teaspoon of butter, lightly grease two baking sheets.

Sift the flour and icing [confectioners'] sugar into a mixing bowl. With a table knife, cut the remaining butter into small pieces and add it to the mixture.

Using your hands, mix the flour and butter together to make a smooth dough.

With the knife, stir in the egg yolk and 2 tablespoons of the cream. Mix very well and form the dough into a ball. Cover the dough with greaseproof or waxed paper and place it in the refrigerator to chill for 30 minutes.

Preheat the oven to fairly hot 375°F (Gas Mark 5, 190°C).

Divide the dough into two equal pieces. On a floured surface, roll out each piece into a 9-inch circle.

Place the circles on the prepared baking sheets and place them in the oven. Bake for 12 to 15 minutes or until the edges of the shortcakes are golden brown.

Remove the sheets from the oven and carefully transfer the shortcakes to a wire rack to cool.

Meanwhile, thinly slice the strawberries. In a medium-sized mixing bowl, beat the remaining cream and the sugar with a wire whisk or rotary beater until the mixture forms stiff peaks.

Lightly fold the strawberries into the cream. Spoon the mixture into a heap in the centre of one of the shortcakes.

With a sharp knife, cut the other circle into eight equal triangles. Pile the triangles up against the strawberry mixture and serve at once.

Strawberry Ziggurat

   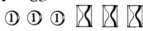

Named after the Ziggurat temple built in ancient Babylonia, Strawberry Ziggurat makes a very impressive and decorative dessert, ideal for summer buffet parties.

8-10 SERVINGS

7 egg whites
14 oz. [1¾ cups] castor sugar

FILLING

1 pint double cream [2½ cups heavy cream]
4 tablespoons orange-flavoured liqueur
2 lb. strawberries, hulled and washed

Preheat the oven to very cool 275°F (Gas Mark 1, 140°C).

Cut out a circle of non-stick silicone paper 9-inches in diameter and place it on a baking sheet.

Cut out another circle of non-stick silicone paper 5⅜-inches in diameter and place it on a second baking sheet.

In a medium-sized mixing bowl, beat 4 egg whites together with a wire whisk or rotary beater until they form stiff peaks. Add 4 teaspoons of the sugar and continue beating for 1 minute.

Using the side of a metal spoon as a cutting edge, fold in 8 ounces [1 cup] of the remaining sugar.

Spoon the mixture into a forcing bag fitted with a large plain nozzle.

Pipe the mixture on to the paper circles on the baking sheets, covering them completely.

Place the baking sheets in the centre of the oven and bake for 1 hour or until the meringues are firm and very lightly browned.

Meanwhile, rinse and dry the forcing bag and set it aside.

Remove the baking sheets from the oven. Carefully transfer the meringues from the baking sheets to a wire rack. Set aside to cool.

Cut out three more circles of non-stick silicone paper: 7⅜-inches, 4⅜-inches and 2½-inches in diameter. Place the largest circle on one baking sheet and the other two circles, well spaced, on the second baking sheet. Set aside.

In a medium-sized mixing bowl, beat the remaining egg whites with a wire whisk or rotary beater until they form stiff peaks. Add 1 tablespoon of the remaining sugar and beat for 1 minute.

Using the side of a metal spoon as a cutting edge, fold in the remaining sugar.

Spoon the mixture into the forcing bag and pipe it on to the paper circles on the baking sheets, covering them completely.

Place the baking sheets in the centre of the oven and bake for 1 hour or until the meringues are firm and light brown.

Remove the baking sheets from the oven and carefully transfer the meringues to a wire rack. Leave them to cool.

Meanwhile, make the filling. In a large mixing bowl, beat the cream and liqueur together with a wire whisk or rotary beater until they form stiff peaks.

Carefully peel off the silicone paper from the meringue circles. Discard the paper.

Place the largest meringue circle on a large, flat serving plate. Spread a thick layer of the cream mixture over the circle to cover it completely. Cover the cream with some of the strawberries, standing them broad base down.

Place the second largest circle over the strawberries. Spread a layer of cream over it and cover with strawberries.

Continue making layers until you come to the smallest circle.

Spread the remaining cream on the bottom of the smallest circle and place it on top of the pyramid.

Place the ziggurat in the refrigerator and chill for 30 minutes before serving.

Simple to make, stunning to look at, Strawberries Romanoff makes the perfect dessert for a special lunch or dinner party.

Tipsy Pudding

☆☆　①①①◪◪

Rich with whisky and sherry, Tipsy Pudding makes a splendidly impressive dessert for a dinner party.

6 SERVINGS

1 teaspoon vegetable oil
3 eggs
3 oz. [⅜ cup] castor sugar
3 oz. [¾ cup] flour, sifted
½ teaspoon vanilla essence
2 tablespoons cornflour [cornstarch], sifted
8 oz. cherry jam
3 fl. oz. [⅜ cup] whisky
3 fl. oz. [⅜ cup] sherry

TOPPING
2 egg yolks
1 teaspoon cornflour [cornstarch]
1 tablespoon sugar
¼ teaspoon vanilla essence
10 fl. oz. [1¼ cups] milk, scalded
10 fl. oz. double cream [1¼ cups heavy cream], stiffly whipped
2 oz. [½ cup] almonds, blanched, split and lightly toasted

Preheat the oven to hot 425°F (Gas Mark 7, 220°C).

This impressive Tipsy Pudding contains whisky and sherry and makes a special treat for dinner!

Line a 10- x 16-inch Swiss [jelly] roll tin with non-stick silicone paper or foil. If you use foil, grease it with the teaspoon of vegetable oil.

Put the eggs and sugar in a medium-sized heatproof mixing bowl. Place the bowl over a pan half-filled with hot water. Set the pan over low heat.

Using a wire whisk or rotary beater, beat the eggs and sugar together until the mixture is thick and makes a ribbon trail on itself when the whisk is lifted.

Remove the bowl from the saucepan. Using a metal spoon or spatula, fold in the flour and the vanilla essence.

Pour the batter into the prepared tin and smooth it down with a knife.

Place the tin in the oven and bake for 8 minutes, or until a skewer inserted into the centre of the cake comes out clean. Remove the tin from the oven. Dust a working surface with the cornflour [cornstarch]. Reverse the cake out on to the working surface. Remove the silicone paper or foil from the bottom of the cake.

Using a knife, spread the jam evenly over the surface of the cake. Roll it up Swiss [jelly] roll style and place it in a long, deep serving dish. Set it aside.

When the roll has cooled to room temperature, pour the whisky and sherry over the surface.

To make the topping, in a heatproof bowl, beat the egg yolks, cornflour [cornstarch], sugar and vanilla essence together with a wire whisk or rotary beater.

Beat in the hot milk. Place the bowl over a pan of simmering water and cook, stirring constantly with a wooden spoon, until the custard thickens and coats the back of the spoon.

Remove the bowl from the heat and pour the custard over the cake. Chill the dish in the refrigerator for 1 hour.

Remove the cake from the refrigerator. Using a palette knife, spread the cream over the top and sides of the cake and stick in the split almonds all over the surface. Serve immediately.

Trifle

☆☆　①①①◪◪◪

This luscious dessert should be served in

small quantities after a light meal.

4-6 SERVINGS

6 trifle sponge squares [6 small
stale sponge cakes], each sliced
into two layers
2 fl. oz. [¼ cup] orange-flavoured
liqueur
2 tablespoons fresh orange juice
10 oz. [1¼ cups] sugar
10 fl. oz. [1¼ cups] custard
4 large oranges, peeled, white pith
removed and thinly sliced
5 fl. oz. double cream [⅝ cup heavy
cream], stiffly whipped

Place the sponge slices in one layer in a
large dish. Sprinkle over the liqueur and

orange juice and set aside for 30 minutes
or until all the liquid has been absorbed.

In a heavy saucepan, dissolve the sugar
over low heat, shaking the pan occasionally. Increase the heat to moderate
and boil the syrup, shaking the pan
occasionally, until it turns a rich golden
brown.

Remove the pan from the heat. Place it
in a bowl of hot water to keep the
caramel hot.

Arrange one-third of the soaked sponge
slices in a medium-sized glass serving
dish. Spoon over one-third of the custard,
smoothing it over evenly with the back
of a spoon. Lay one-third of the orange
slices over the custard to cover it com-

*This unusual version of the classic
British Trifle contains oranges,
orange liqueur and caramel.*

pletely. Trickle over one-third of the
caramel in a thin stream.

Continue making layers in the same
way, ending with a layer of caramel-
coated orange slices.

Place the trifle in the refrigerator and
chill it for 2 hours.

Fill a small forcing bag, fitted with a
star-shaped nozzle, with the cream.

Remove the trifle from the refrigerator
and pipe the cream over the top in
decorative swirls. Serve immediately.

Vacherin aux Noisettes

Vacherin aux Noisettes is a scrumptious combination of hazelnut-flavoured meringue enclosing a chocolate-cream filling and topped with fresh, juicy apricots.

4-6 SERVINGS

2 teaspoons butter
4 egg whites
8 oz. [1 cup] castor sugar
½ teaspoon vanilla essence
4 oz. [⅔ cup] ground hazelnuts
4 oz. dark [semi-sweet] cooking chocolate, cut into pieces
2 tablespoons water
8 oz. double cream [1 cup heavy cream], stiffly whipped
3 tablespoons chopped hazelnuts, toasted
4 fresh apricots, blanched, peeled, halved and stoned

Preheat the oven to moderate 350°F (Gas Mark 4, 180°C). With the butter, lightly grease two 7-inch loose-bottomed sandwich tins and set them aside.

In a large mixing bowl, beat the egg whites with a wire whisk or rotary beater until they form stiff peaks. Beat in 2 tablespoons of the sugar and continue beating until the peaks are very stiff and glossy. (You should be able to turn the bowl upside down without the mixture falling out.) Using a metal spoon, fold in the remaining sugar. Stir in the vanilla essence and fold in the ground hazelnuts.

Pour half the meringue mixture into each of the prepared tins and smooth with a flat-bladed knife. Place the tins in the oven and bake for 30 to 40 minutes or until the meringues are light gold and firm. Remove the tins from the oven and allow the meringue cakes to cool in the tins for 5 minutes. Remove the meringues from the tins, carefully transfer them to a wire rack and leave them to cool completely.

Meanwhile, place the chocolate and water in a heatproof bowl placed over a pan of hot water. Set the pan over low heat and cook, stirring occasionally, until the chocolate has melted. Remove the pan from the heat and the bowl from the pan. Set aside to cool.

When the chocolate is cool but not set, using a metal spoon, fold in half of the cream and the toasted hazelnuts.

With a knife, spread the filling over one of the meringue cakes. Place the other cake over the top.

Wash the knife and use it to spread the remaining cream over the top of the vacherin. Arrange the apricot halves decoratively over the cream and serve immediately.

Yogurt Crumb Cake

Yogurt Crumb Cake, a combination of yogurt, cream and apricots on a crunchy biscuit [cracker] base, makes a delicious and decorative dessert.

8 SERVINGS

4 oz. [½ cup] plus 1 teaspoon butter, melted
8 oz. crushed digestive biscuits [2 cups crushed graham crackers]
1 teaspoon ground cinnamon
10 fl. oz. [1¼ cups] yogurt
16 fl. oz. double cream [2 cups heavy cream]
1 tablespoon lemon juice
2 oz. [¼ cup] castor sugar,
1 lb. fresh apricots blanched, peeled, halved, stoned and finely chopped
½ oz. gelatine, dissolved in 4 tablespoons hot water
2 oz. chocolate caraque
2 oz. [½ cup] slivered almonds, toasted

Lightly grease a 9-inch loose-bottomed cake tin with the teaspoon of butter. Set aside.

In a medium-sized mixing bowl, combine the crushed biscuits [crackers], the remaining melted butter and the cinnamon with a wooden spoon. Line the base of the cake tin with the biscuit [cracker] mixture, pressing it firmly against the bottom of the tin with your fingers or with the back of the wooden spoon. Set aside.

In a medium-sized bowl, beat the yogurt, half of the cream, the lemon juice and the sugar together with a wooden spoon until the mixture is smooth and creamy. Stir in the apricots. Beat in the dissolved gelatine mixture. Set the yogurt mixture aside in a cool place for 20 minutes or until it is on the point of setting.

Using a large metal spoon, spoon the mixture on to the biscuit [cracker] base. Place the tin in the refrigerator and chill for 30 minutes or until the mixture has set.

Meanwhile, in a medium-sized mixing bowl, beat the remaining double [heavy] cream with a wire whisk or rotary beater until it forms stiff peaks.

Remove the cake tin from the refrigerator and carefully spoon the whipped cream over the top of the cake, making decorative, swirling patterns with the back of the spoon.

Sprinkle the chocolate caraque and toasted almonds over the cream. Serve immediately or chill in the refrigerator until required.

Zuccotto

ITALIAN PUMPKIN-SHAPED CREAM AND SPONGE DESSERT

Zuccotto is a well-known Italian dessert which resembles a pumpkin in shape. Serve this rich, spectacular-looking dessert at a special dinner party.

8-10 SERVINGS

1 pint double cream [2½ cups heavy cream], beaten until stiff
1 oz. [¼ cup] plus 2 tablespoons icing [confectioners'] sugar
2 oz. [½ cup] hazelnuts, toasted
8 oz. fresh cherries, halved and stoned
4 oz. dark [semi-sweet] dessert chocolate, finely chopped or grated
2 fl. oz. [¼ cup] brandy
2 fl. oz. [¼ cup] orange-flavoured liqueur
2 x 8-inch chocolate sponge cakes, sliced in 2 horizontally
2 tablespoons cocoa powder

In a small mixing bowl, combine the cream and 1 ounce icing sugar [¼ cup confectioners' sugar]. Using a metal spoon, fold in the hazelnuts, cherries and chocolate. Chill the bowl in the refrigerator.

In a small mixing bowl, mix together the brandy and orange-flavoured liqueur and set aside.

Line a 2-pint [1½-quart] pudding basin with three-quarters of the sponge, cutting it into pieces with a sharp knife so that it fits the shape of the basin. Sprinkle the brandy mixture over the sponge lining.

Remove the cream mixture from the refrigerator and spoon it into the sponge case. Use the remaining sponge to cover it. Chill the basin in the refrigerator for 2 hours.

Remove the basin from the refrigerator. Run a knife around the edge of the pudding to loosen it. Invert a serving plate over the basin and, holding the two firmly together, reverse them. The zuccotto should slide out easily.

Sprinkle half of the remaining icing [confectioners'] sugar neatly over one-quarter of the pudding. Sprinkle half the cocoa powder over a second quarter, then repeat this over the other half of the pudding so that the zuccotto has 4 alternating segments of colour.

Serve immediately.

Zuccotto is an unusual-shaped Italian dessert containing cream, cherries, chocolate and liqueurs. Serve as a rich finale to a special dinner.

Apple Pudding

A delicious, sustaining dish of Scandinavian origin, this pudding is the perfect dessert for either a dinner party or a family meal. If zwieback is not available use a dark, dry brown bread.

4 SERVINGS

4 oz. [1 cup] zwieback, crushed
½ teaspoon ground allspice
1½ oz. [3 tablespoons] butter, melted
1½ lb. thick apple puree
½ teaspoon ground cinnamon
12 fl. oz. double cream [1½ cups heavy cream]
8 oz. white grapes, coated with egg white and sugar

In a mixing bowl, combine the zwieback, allspice and butter. Using one-half of the mixture, line the bottom of a medium-sized round cake tin with a removable base. Top with half the apple purée and sprinkle over half the cinnamon.

In a second medium-sized mixing bowl, beat the cream with a wire whisk or rotary beater until it forms stiff peaks. Spoon about one-half of the cream over the apple puree and cinnamon. Top with the remaining crushed zwieback, apple purée and cinnamon and then with the remaining cream. Bring it up into decorative swirls with a flat-bladed knife. Arrange the white grapes decoratively over the top of the mixture and chill in the refrigerator for 1 hour.

To serve, remove the tin from the refrigerator, remove the pudding from the tin and place it on a serving dish. Serve at once.

Banana Cream Pie

This delicious and inexpensive American banana pie is made with shortcrust pastry and topped with meringue.

6 SERVINGS

PASTRY
6 oz. [1½ cups] flour
¼ teaspoon salt
3¼ oz. [½ cup] vegetable fat or lard
2 tablespoons iced water
FILLING
3 egg yolks

Apple Pudding, a mixture of apple purée, zwieback and cream, makes a delightfully inexpensive dessert.

3 oz. [⅜ cup] castor sugar
¼ teaspoon salt
2 tablespoons cornflour [cornstarch]
1 tablespoon butter
16 fl. oz. [2 cups] milk
1 teaspoon vanilla essence
2 ripe bananas, peeled and sliced
TOPPING
3 egg whites
6 oz. [¾ cup] castor sugar
2 tablespoons shredded almonds

Sift the flour and salt into a mixing bowl. Add the vegetable fat and with your fingertips rub it into the flour until it resembles coarse breadcrumbs. Add a tablespoon of iced water and mix and knead the dough until it is smooth. Add more water if the dough is too dry. Roll the dough into a ball, cover it and chill it in the refrigerator for 30 minutes.

Preheat the oven to fairly hot 400°F (Gas Mark 6, 200°C).

On a floured board, roll the dough out and line a 9-inch pie tin. Put the lined pie tin in the refrigerator for 10 minutes.

When you remove the pie tin from the refrigerator, prick the dough with a fork, line it with greaseproof paper and weigh it down with dried beans or peas. Bake the shell for 10 minutes.

Remove the greaseproof paper and bake for 5 minutes more, or until the shell is golden.

Reset the oven to cool 300°F (Gas Mark 2, 150°C).

To prepare the filling, beat the egg yolks in a heatproof bowl with a whisk. Gradually beat in the sugar, salt, cornflour [cornstarch] and butter.

Put the milk in a small saucepan and, over moderate heat, bring it almost to boiling point. Pour slowly on to the egg mixture, stirring continuously. Place the bowl in a pan of boiling water and cook the custard until it thickens. Cool the custard and then add the vanilla essence. Arrange the banana slices in the pie shell. Pour the custard over them.

Beat the egg whites in a small bowl with a rotary beater until they are stiff. Beat in one tablespoon of sugar and then fold in the remaining sugar. Pile the meringue on top of the custard and spread to cover completely. Sprinkle with the almonds and bake for 15 to 20 minutes or until the meringue is lightly browned. Serve cold.

Fig Flutter

This light, steamed pudding must be served as soon as it is ready because it falls as it cools. Serve with custard.

3 oz. [⅜ cup] plus 1 teaspoon butter
5 slices of white bread, crusts
    removed, cut into pieces
10 fl. oz. [1¼ cups] milk
6 egg yolks
4 oz. [½ cup] sugar
3 oz. [½ cup] ground almonds
½ teaspoon grated nutmeg
5 oz. [1 cup] dried figs, stalks
    removed and chopped
½ teaspoon almond essence
6 egg whites

Grease a 2-pint [1½-quart] soufflé dish
with the teaspoon of butter. Tie a double
band of greaseproof or waxed paper 5
inches wide around the soufflé dish.

In a small saucepan, combine the bread
and milk over low heat. Simmer, stirring
occasionally, until the bread has blended
into the milk. Remove the pan from the
heat and stir in the remaining butter until
it has melted. Set aside.

In a large mixing bowl, beat the egg
yolks and sugar together with a wire
whisk or rotary beater until the mixture
is pale and fluffy. Stir in the almonds,
nutmeg, figs, almond essence and the
milk and bread mixture.

In another large mixing bowl, beat the
egg whites with a wire whisk or rotary
beater until they are stiff. With a metal

spoon, carefully fold the egg whites into
the egg yolk mixture.

Pour the mixture into the soufflé dish.
Place the dish in the top part of a steamer,
the lower half of which is three-quarters
filled with hot water. Cover and place
over high heat. Bring the water to the
boil. Reduce the heat to moderate and
steam the pudding for 50 minutes.

Remove the pudding from the steamer
and serve immediately.

Honeydew Melon with Blackcurrant Iced Mousse

*A cool dessert to finish a summer dinner
party, Honeydew Melon with Blackcurrant
Iced Mousse is superb.*

10 fl. oz. [1¼ cups] blackcurrant juice
5 fl. oz. [⅝ cup] water
2 oz. [¼ cup] sugar
    grated rind and juice of 1 lemon
½ oz. gelatine, dissolved in 2
    tablespoons hot water
1 egg white
1 large honeydew melon

Set the thermostat of the refrigerator to
its coldest setting.

In a saucepan, combine the black-

*Honeydew Melon with Blackcurrant
Iced Mousse.*

currant juice, water, sugar and lemon
rind. Bring to the boil over moderately
high heat and boil for 4 minutes. Remove
the pan from the heat and stir in the
lemon juice and dissolved gelatine. Pour
the mixture through a strainer into a
freezer tray. Place the freezer tray in the
frozen food storage compartment of the
refrigerator and chill for 30 minutes.

In a small bowl, beat the egg white
with a wire whisk or rotary beater until it
forms stiff peaks. Whisk the blackcurrant
mixture into the egg white. Spoon the
mixture back into the freezer tray and
return to the storage compartment. Freeze
the mixture for a further 1 hour.

Remove the freezer tray from the
refrigerator and turn the blackcurrant
mixture into the mixing bowl. Whisk for
1 minute. Return the mixture to the
freezer tray and replace it in the storage
compartment. Continue whisking every
hour for 4 hours, then leave the iced
mousse to freeze overnight.

With a sharp knife, slice the melon
crossways into six slices. Scoop out the
seeds and place the slices on individual
plates. Spoon the mousse into the centre
of each piece. Serve at once.

Cold Lemon Soufflé

A light, refreshing dessert, Cold Lemon Soufflé is particularly good after a heavy meal. The soufflé looks most attractive if it is set in a 6-inch soufflé dish, tied with a raised collar of greaseproof or waxed paper. The paper is removed after the soufflé is set and the top of the soufflé may then be decorated with chopped or slivered nuts, biscuits [cookies] or glacé cherries and cream. The soufflé may also be set in a decorative glass or china serving bowl or it may be used as a flan filling.

6 SERVINGS

5 egg yolks
4 oz. [½ cup] castor sugar
  finely grated rind and juice of
  3 lemons
½ oz. gelatine, dissolved in 4
  tablespoons hot water
10 fl. oz. double cream [1¼ cups
  heavy cream]
5 egg whites

In a medium-sized heatproof mixing bowl, combine the egg yolks and sugar. Put the bowl over a saucepan half full of hot water. Place the pan over moderate heat and, using a wire whisk or rotary beater, beat the mixture for 15 to 20 minutes or until it is thick.

Add the lemon rind and juice and continue beating until well mixed and the mixture makes a ribbon trail on itself when the whisk is lifted.

Alternatively, beat the egg yolks, sugar and lemon rind for 5 minutes or until thick in an electric mixer. Add the lemon juice to the egg mixture and continue beating for 15 to 20 minutes or until the mixture makes a ribbon trail on itself when the beater is lifted.

Remove the bowl from the pan and set it in a large bowl or baking dish containing cold water. Continue whisking until the mixture and the bowl are both quite cold.

Pour in the gelatine and stir well.

In a medium-sized mixing bowl, beat the cream with a wire whisk or rotary beater until it is thick but not stiff, then carefully fold it into the egg and lemon mixture. Place the bowl in the refrigerator and chill the mixture for 45 minutes to 1 hour, or until it is cold but not quite set.

In a large bowl, beat the egg whites with a wire whisk until they form stiff peaks. Using a large metal spoon, carefully fold the egg whites into the soufflé mixture. Turn the mixture into a soufflé dish or serving bowl and place in the refrigerator to set for 4 hours or overnight before serving.

Mixed Fruit Cream

A refreshing dessert, Mixed Fruit Cream takes only a few minutes to prepare and makes a delightful ending to a summer meal.

4 SERVINGS

8 oz. cream cheese
5 fl. oz. single cream [⅝ cup light
  cream]
1 tablespoon light rum
2 tablespoons sugar
1 medium-sized pear, peeled,
  cored and finely chopped
2 medium-sized peaches, peeled,
  stoned and finely chopped
¼ medium-sized melon, peeled,
  seeded and finely chopped
1 oz. chocolate, grated
4 oz. grapes, halved and seeded

In a medium-sized mixing bowl, beat the cream cheese, cream and rum together with a wooden spoon until they are blended. Stir in the sugar. Add the pear, peaches and melon and mix well to blend.

Spoon the mixture into four individual serving bowls or dessert glasses. Sprinkle the grated chocolate over the top, and arrange the grapes in a circle around the edge of each serving bowl. Serve immediately.

October Cobbler

A traditional English fruit pie, October Cobbler may be made with any fruit plentiful in the autumn — blackberries, apples, pears, damson plums, etc. Serve October Cobbler hot, with whipped cream.

4 SERVINGS

PASTRY
6 oz. [1½ cups] flour
⅛ teaspoon salt
3 oz. [⅜ cup] butter
2 tablespoons sugar
1 small egg
1 to 2 tablespoons iced water
1 egg yolk, well beaten with 2
  tablespoons milk
FILLING
1 lb. fruit, prepared and
  washed
2 medium-sized tart cooking
  apples, peeled, cored and chopped
3 tablespoons water
2 oz. [⅓ cup] soft brown sugar
  grated rind of 1 small orange
¼ teaspoon ground cinnamon

Cooling, tangy Cold Lemon Soufflé makes a beautifully elegant end to a heavy meal.

2 teaspoons arrowroot dissolved in
  1 tablespoon orange juice

First, make the pastry. Sift the flour and salt into a medium-sized mixing bowl. Add the butter and cut it into small pieces with a table knife. With your fingers, rub the butter into the flour until the mixture resembles fine breadcrumbs. Stir in 1 tablespoon of the sugar.

In a small mixing bowl, beat the egg and 1 tablespoon of the water together with a fork. Make a well in the centre of the flour mixture and pour in the egg and water mixture. With a knife, quickly mix the ingredients into a firm dough. Add a little more of the water if the dough is too dry. With your fingertips, lightly knead the dough until it is smooth.

Shape the dough into a ball and wrap it in greaseproof or waxed paper. Chill the dough in the refrigerator for 30 minutes.

Meanwhile, make the filling. Place the fruit, apples, water, sugar, orange rind and cinnamon in a medium-sized saucepan. Set the pan over moderately high heat and bring the mixture to the boil, stirring constantly. Reduce the heat to low, cover the pan and simmer, stirring occasionally, for 6 to 8 minutes or until

62

the fruit is tender.

Stir in the dissolved arrowroot and cook the mixture, stirring constantly, for 3 minutes, or until the liquid has thickened.

Remove the pan from the heat. Spoon the fruit mixture into a medium-sized pie dish. Set aside.

Preheat the oven to fairly hot 400°F (Gas Mark 6, 200°C).

Remove the dough from the refrigerator and place it on a lightly floured board. With a floured rolling pin, roll out the dough into a circle approximately ¼-inch thick.

Using a 2-inch round fluted pastry cutter, cut the dough into circles. Gather the remaining dough into a ball and knead it lightly until it is smooth. Roll the dough out into a strip approximately ⅛-inch thick. With a sharp knife, trim the dough strip to make it ½-inch wide.

Wet the rim of the pie dish with a little cold water. Place the dough strip on the rim of the dish to cover it completely. Trim off any excess dough with a sharp knife and press the ends of the strip together to seal them.

Place the dough circles over the dough strip, pressing them down lightly. The circles should overlap slightly forming a border around the pie and leaving a gap

in the middle to expose the filling.

Lightly prick the circles with a fork and brush them with the egg yolk and milk mixture. Sprinkle over the remaining tablespoon of sugar.

Place the cobbler in the centre of the oven and bake for 20 to 30 minutes, or until the pastry is cooked and golden brown.

Remove the cobbler from the oven and serve immediately, straight from the dish.

Peach Dessert

This Peach Dessert makes a wonderfully light and refreshing ending for a summer lunch or dinner.

4 SERVINGS

4 fresh peaches, blanched, peeled, halved and stoned
3 tablespoons double [heavy] cream
1 tablespoon castor sugar
¼ teaspoon vanilla essence
1 oz. dark dessert chocolate, finely grated
4 tablespoons blanched slivered almonds

Arrange two peach halves, rounded sides

down, in each of 4 individual dessert dishes. Set aside.

In a medium-sized mixing bowl, whisk the cream, sugar and vanilla essence together with a wire whisk or rotary beater until the mixture forms soft peaks. With a spoon or spatula, gently fold half of the chocolate and half of the almonds into the cream mixture. Place a little of the mixture in each peach half.

Sprinkle each dish with equal amounts of the remaining grated chocolate and almonds. Chill in the refrigerator for at least 1 hour before serving.

Raspberry Pudding

Raspberry Pudding is a light and pleasant dessert to make when fresh raspberries are in season. Serve it with lots of whipped cream.

4 SERVINGS

2 oz. [¼ cup] plus 1 teaspoon butter
5 fl. oz. [⅝ cup] water
6 oz. [1½ cups] flour
3 eggs
1 tablespoon finely grated orange rind
1 lb. fresh raspberries, washed and hulled
3 tablespoons castor sugar
1 teaspoon icing [confectioners'] sugar

Using the teaspoon of butter, lightly grease a baking sheet. Set aside. Preheat the oven to fairly hot 400°F (Gas Mark 6, 200°C).

In a large saucepan, bring the water to the boil over moderate heat. Add the butter. When the butter has melted, remove the pan from the heat and beat in the flour. Continue beating until the mixture pulls away from the sides of the pan.

Beat the eggs into the mixture one by one, beating each one into the dough until it is well blended before adding the next. When the eggs have been completely absorbed, the mixture should be thick and glossy. Stir in the orange rind.

Spread one-quarter of the mixture on the baking sheet to make a 7-inch circle. Spoon the remaining mixture around the edge of the circle to make a case.

Put the raspberries and sugar into the pastry case. Place the baking sheet in the oven and bake for 40 minutes or until the pastry has risen and is deep golden brown in colour. Remove the baking sheet from the oven and transfer the pudding to a serving dish. Sprinkle the pudding with the icing [confectioners'] sugar and serve immediately.

Viennese Coffee Cake

This decorative and delicious dessert cake is very easy to make.

4 SERVINGS

4 oz. [½ cup] butter
4 oz. [1 cup] self-raising flour
4 oz. [½ cup] plus 2 teaspoons sugar
2 eggs
2 oz. [½ cup] crushed walnuts plus a few halves for decoration
6 fl. oz. [¾ cup] strong black coffee
2 fl. oz. [¼ cup] brandy
10 fl. oz. double cream [1¼ cups heavy cream]
½ teaspoon vanilla essence

Preheat the oven to moderate 350°F (Gas Mark 4, 180°C). Using a little of the butter, grease a 7-inch cake tin, then dust with a little flour.

In a bowl, beat the butter with a wooden spoon until it is soft. Add 4 ounces [½ cup] sugar and beat until the mixture is creamy. Add the eggs, one at a time, with 1 tablespoon of flour. Beat to mix and then fold in the remaining flour and the crushed walnuts. Turn the batter into the prepared cake tin. Bake for 50 minutes, or until a skewer inserted into the centre of the cake comes out clean.

Remove the cake from the tin and place on a rack to cool. Mix the coffee and brandy. Put the cake back in the cake tin and slowly pour the coffee and brandy over it. When all the liquid has been absorbed, turn out on to a dish.

Whip the cream with the remaining 2 teaspoons of the sugar and the vanilla essence. Using a spatula, spread the cream in whirls over the cake to cover it completely. Decorate with walnut halves.

Yeast Buckwheat Pancakes with Blackberries and Sour Cream

Yeast Buckwheat Pancakes with Blackberries and Sour Cream makes a really special dessert.

6 SERVINGS

½ oz. fresh yeast
2 oz. [¼ cup] plus 1 teaspoon sugar
10 fl. oz. [1¼ cups] milk, lukewarm
10 oz. [2½ cups] buckwheat flour
¼ teaspoon salt
2 eggs, lightly beaten
1 oz. [2 tablespoons] butter, melted
2 oz. [¼ cup] butter
2 tablespoons icing [confectioners'] sugar
1 lb. blackberries, washed and drained
10 fl. oz. [1¼ cups] sour cream

Yeast Buckwheat Pancakes with Blackberries and Sour Cream.

Crumble the yeast into a small bowl and mash in 1 teaspoon of the sugar with a fork. Add 2 tablespoons of the milk and cream the mixture to form a smooth paste. Set the bowl aside in a warm, draught-free place for 15 to 20 minutes or until the mixture is puffed up.

In a large mixing bowl, combine the flour and salt. Make a well in the centre and pour in the yeast, the remaining milk and sugar, the eggs and melted butter.

Using your fingers, gradually draw the flour mixture into the liquid. Continue mixing until all the flour is incorporated and the mixture is smooth.

Set the batter aside in a warm draught-free place for 30 minutes.

In a large frying-pan, melt half of the butter over high heat. Drop tablespoonfuls of the batter into the pan and fry, turning once, for 30 seconds on each side or until the pancakes are golden brown. Transfer the pancakes to a warmed serving plate and keep hot while you fry the remaining batter in the same way.

When all the pancakes have been fried, sprinkle over the icing [confectioners'] sugar. Place the blackberries in one bowl and the sour cream in another and serve immediately, with the pancakes.